Armies of Plantagenet England, 1135–1337

Armies of Plantagenet England, 1135–1337

The Scottish and Welsh Wars and Continental Campaigns

Gabriele Esposito

Pen & Sword
MILITARY

First published in Great Britain in 2022
by Pen & Sword Military
An imprint of Pen & Sword Books Limited
47 Church Street
Barnsley
South Yorkshire
S70 2AS

ISBN 978 1 39900 835 8

A CIP catalogue record for this book is
available from the British Library

Typeset in Adobe Caslon
by Mac Style

Printed and bound in India by Replika Press Pvt. Ltd.

MIX
Paper from
responsible sources
FSC
www.fsc.org
FSC® C016779

Pen & Sword Books Limited incorporates the imprints of Atlas,
Archaeology, Aviation, Discovery, Family History, Fiction, History, Maritime,
Military, Military Classics, Politics, Select, Transport, True Crime, Air World,
Frontline Publishing, Leo Cooper, Remember When, Seaforth Publishing,
The Praetorian Press, Wharncliffe Local History, Wharncliffe Transport,
Wharncliffe True Crime and White Owl.

For a complete list of Pen & Sword titles please contact
PEN & SWORD BOOKS LIMITED
47 Church Street, Barnsley, South Yorkshire, S70 2AS, England
E-mail: enquiries@pen-and-sword.co.uk
Website: www. pen-and-sword.co.uk

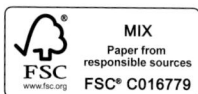

Contents

Gabriele Esposito is a military historian who works as a freelance author and researcher for some of the most important publishing houses in the military history sector. In particular, he is an expert specializing in uniformology: his interests and expertise range from the ancient civilizations to modern post-colonial conflicts. During recent years, he has conducted and published several researches on the military history of the Latin American countries, with special attention on the War of the Triple Alliance and the War of the Pacific. He is among the leading experts on the military history of the Italian Wars of Unification and the Spanish Carlist Wars. His books and essays are published on a regular basis by Osprey Publishing, Winged Hussar Publishing and Libreria Editrice Goriziana; he is also the author of numerous military history articles appearing in specialized magazines like *Ancient Warfare Magazine, Medieval Warfare Magazine, The Armourer, History of War, Guerres et Histoire, Focus Storia* and *Focus Storia Wars*.

Acknowledgements

This book is dedicated to my magnificent parents, Maria Rosaria and Benedetto, for the immense love and fundamental support that they always give me. Their precious advice over many years has helped to make the present book a much better one than it otherwise would be. A very special thanks goes to Philip Sidnell, the commissioning editor of my books for Pen & Sword: his love for history and his passion for publishing are the key factors behind the success of our publications. Many thanks also to the production manager of this title, Matt Jones, for his excellent work and great enthusiasm, and to copy-editor Tony Walton, for his usual superb work on my manuscripts. A very special mention goes to the brilliant re-enactment groups that collaborated with their photos to the creation of this book: without the incredible work of research by their members, the final result of this publication would have not been the same. As a result, I want to express my deep gratitude to the following living history associations: 'Confraternita del Leone/ Historia Viva' from Italy and 'Sirotci' from Poland.

Introduction

The English monarchs belonging to the House of Plantagenet played a fundamental role in the history of the British Isles during the Middle Ages, controlling England for a very long period during which the political situation of their kingdom changed dramatically. After the Norman Conquest from 1066 onwards, the English lands gradually lost their Saxon character and became much more similar to continental Europe than previously. The Normans brought feudalism to the British Isles, together with a new model of centralized monarchy, thereby changing the administrative and social structures of England forever. After a few decades, however, the new royal family initiated by William the Conqueror disappeared due to the lack of direct heirs, and thus the Kingdom of England entered a chaotic phase characterized by civil conflicts and the search for a new royal house that could assume control over the turbulent English lands. This historical period, known as 'The Anarchy', began in 1135, ending only in 1154 when the first Plantagenet was crowned as monarch of England. The new royal family retained power over its kingdom for more than three centuries until the outbreak of the War of the Roses. During this long period, the Plantagenet kings fought a series of conflicts, which can be grouped into three main categories: wars fought against the French monarchy in continental Europe, those fought in the British Isles against the Celtic nations (Wales, Scotland and Ireland), and civil conflicts fought in England against rebel aristocrats. Sometimes, wars belonging to two different categories could take place at the same time: it was not uncommon, in fact, to see the English nobles rebelling against their king while the latter was campaigning on the borders of his realm or in France. The historical period covered in this book ends with the year 1337, which marked a real turning point in the history of England since it saw the beginning of the Hundred Years' War with France. This was just the latest in a series of medieval conflicts fought between England and France, but unlike the previous wars of the early Plantagenet period, it was conducted on a massive scale and was to last for more than a century.

In the first two centuries of their rule over England, the Plantagenets demonstrated that they were a very warlike dynasty: their main political objective was to conquer a large portion of the British Isles by defeating the political entities bordering with

England. By the end of the period taken into account – i.e. by the middle of the fourteenth century – they had only partially achieved their ambitious objectives. For while Wales had been conquered thanks to the military efforts of Edward I, most of Ireland and the whole of Scotland remained fully independent. This situation would remain more or less unchanged well after the end of the Hundred Years' War, highlighting that the defeat of the Celtic nations was not as easy to achieve as the Plantagenets had initially expected.

In this book we will cover the history, organization and equipment of the English armies that fought the many conflicts of the early Plantagenet period, paying special attention to the wars fought by England against Wales, Scotland and Ireland, while at the same time providing a detailed overview of the more minor conflicts that saw the Plantagenet monarchs campaigning in France. These were merely an anticipation of the longer war that would start in 1337, but sometimes had significant consequences for the history of England. For instance, Richard the Lionheart, the most famous of the Plantagenet kings, was killed while besieging a castle in France, and his infamous brother, John, was largely forced to sign the Magna Carta due to the defeat that he had suffered at the hands of the French in the Battle of Bouvines (one of the largest pitched battles fought during the age of feudal Europe).

Like their Norman predecessors, the Plantagenets were French aristocrats before becoming monarchs of England. Consequently, they always retained large territorial possessions in continental Europe and remained, in essence, vassals of the King of France. It is clear, however, that a king being the vassal of another king was in a very difficult political position, and it was this that caused most of the Anglo-French conflicts covered in the present work. The most brutal wars of the early Plantagenet period, however, were without doubt the civil conflicts fought against the rebellious nobles. From the beginning of their dynasty, in fact, the concept of 'centralized monarchy' was accepted only with great difficulty by the English aristocrats.

Chapter 1

The Anarchy and the Rise of the Plantagenets

After conquering the Kingdom of England following the Battle of Hastings in 1066, William of Normandy ruled over his new realm until 1087, when he died in France during a minor military campaign. He was succeeded by his third son, who reigned over England as William II until 1100. He was in turn succeeded by Henry I, fourth son of William the Conqueror and thus younger brother of William II and who reigned until 1135 as the last of the Norman monarchs. Henry had just one legitimate son, William Adelin, who was to be his heir both as King of England and Duke of Normandy. In 1106, Henry I had been able to reconquer the French domains inherited from his famous father and thus had reunited (albeit temporarily) the English and French territories of the Normans under the rule of a single monarch. In 1120, however, William Adelin died when the royal vessel known as the 'White Ship' that was transporting the heir to the throne sank en route from Normandy to England. This dynastic tragedy led to the beginning of a complex phase in the history of England.

Henry was by now too old to generate a new male heir. He had a legitimate daughter, Matilda, but in Medieval Europe it was very uncommon for a woman to inherit a throne. Yet having no other choice, during the years that followed 1120, Henry I designated Matilda as his successor, despite the opposition of a good portion of the English nobility. After having been married to Henry V, monarch of the Holy Roman Empire, who died in 1125, Matilda remarried one of the most powerful French nobles, Geoffrey V, Count of Anjou, in 1128. Geoffrey V controlled a vast swathe of territory in north-western France and was one of the King of France's most powerful vassals. The County of Anjou bordered with the Duchy of Normandy, and the Angevins had been the fiercest enemies of the Normans for many years. The border between Normandy and Anjou had been the scene of several battles between the two aristocratic families, and thus Geoffrey V was hated by many of England's Norman nobility. The ageing Henry I tried his best to secure the loyalty of his aristocrats towards Matilda, obliging the English nobles to swear their allegiance to her on three occasions, but such formalities did little to ease the problem. Geoffrey V had very ambitious political plans: he wanted to unite England, Normandy and Anjou into a single Angevin Empire stretching from the southern borders of Scotland to the very heart of France. However, he was impatient, pressing Henry I with his requests. This led to the breaking off of relations between the English king and his daughter Matilda, since Henry understood that the Angevins wanted to occupy Normandy before his death (which did not seem to be imminent). As a result, when a minor revolt broke out in southern Normandy, Matilda and her husband joined the rebels. Henry went to France at the head of a military force with the objective of crushing the rebellious couple, but died in 1135 before encountering them on the field of battle. A succession crisis ensued: Matilda had revolted against her father, but she was still formally the legitimate heir of Henry. Most of the English nobles, however, had no intention of supporting her, because her husband had attacked Normandy and because she was a woman. Consequently, before Matilda and Geoffrey could take the initiative, the English nobles crowned a new Norman king: Stephen of Blois.

Stephen was the son of Adela of Normandy, a daughter of William the Conqueror who had married Stephen Henry of Blois (one of the most powerful nobles of northern France). Stephen was not the eldest son of Stephen Henry of Blois, and thus had no chance of inheriting his father's French territories. As a result, since his childhood he lived at Henry I's court as a client of the king and took part in several of the military campaigns conducted by his uncle. In 1125, Stephen had married Matilda of Boulogne, the daughter and only heir of the Duke of Boulogne. The latter was another very important French aristocrat, who also owned large territorial domains in southern England. With Henry I's death, Stephen of Blois had become a respected member of the English court and his younger brother had risen to prominence after becoming the Bishop of Winchester. Thanks to the support of his wife and brother, as well as of the Norman aristocrats, Stephen was chosen as the new King of England.

Initially, Matilda and Geoffrey were detained in southern Normandy by the ongoing military operations. They made little progress against the royal army that had been raised by Henry I and were unable to reach England to claim the vacant throne. Stephen, however, sailed from Boulogne to his new realm very rapidly. Due to his brother Henry's influence he could count on the support of the Church, and he was acclaimed by the population of London because of Geoffrey's unpopularity. In exchange for the Archbishop of Canterbury's support for his succession to the throne, Stephen granted extensive freedoms and liberties to the Church. Within a few weeks of his coronation, the newly crowned King Stephen was able to obtain the support of all the major nobles, although he soon had to march north in order to defend the borders of his realm. After hearing of Henry I's death, David I of Scotland had attacked northern England in a bid to capture various border fortifications by using to his advantage the political turmoil taking place in London. The Scottish troops obtained a series of minor successes during the early phase of this border conflict, occupying several strongholds along the frontier, together with the larger

KINGDOM OF ENGLAND
(to the Angevins 1154)

Bruges   Ghent

C of FLANDERS

○ Amiens

VASSALS

○ Rouen   Reims

D of NORMANDIE
(to the Angevins 1144)

○ Paris   D of CHAMPAGNE

ROYAL   OF THE

D of BRETAGNE
*(to the son of Henry II
1166)*

Rennes   C of MAINE
○   Le Mans   DOMAIN   ○ Troyes

*(Angevins possessions
to 1144)*   ○ Orleans

Angers   Blois
○

Nantes   Tours   FRENCH   Dijon
○   C of ANJOU   ○   C of BLOIS   ○

C of TOURAINE

Bourges
○

D of BOURGOGNE

POITOU   ○

The Angevin (Platagenet)
possessions in France and
England in XII century   Poitiers   KING

C of LA MARCHE

DUCHY OF   ○
Limoges
○   Clermont
Angouleme   V of LIMOGES   ○

AQUITAINE   C of AUVERGNE

C of PERIGORD

Bordeaux
○
*(to the Angevins by
Eleonor of Aquitaine
1152)*

COUNTY OF

○ Albi   Nimes
○

Auche
○
D of GASCOGNE   ○ Toulouse

TOULOUSE

○ Tarbes
Carcason
○

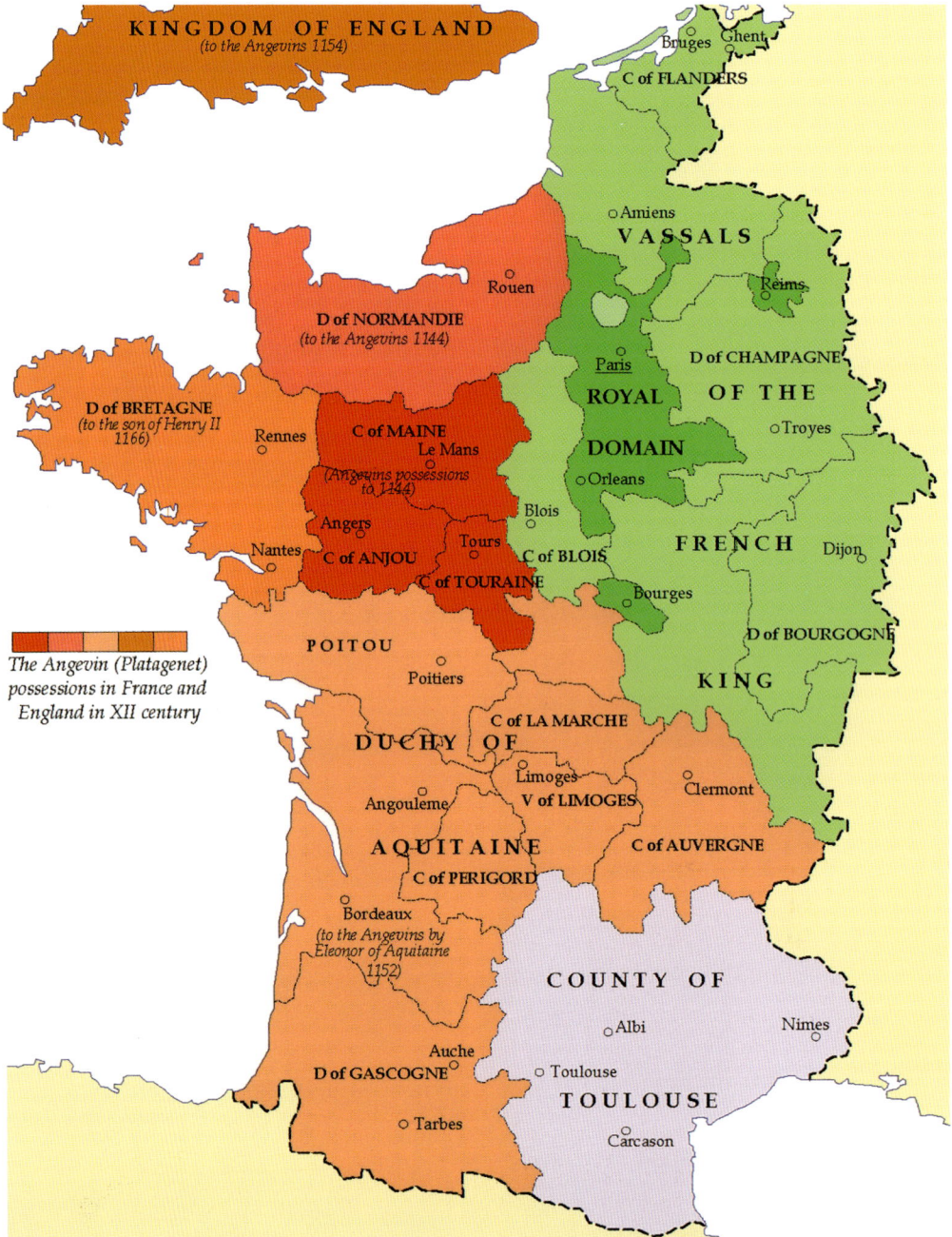

Map of the Angevin Empire at its maximum territorial extent.

centres of Carlisle and Newcastle. At that time the exact border between the Scottish Lowlands and northern England was not precisely defined: David I, for example, considered both Cumberland and Northumbria as part of his personal domains, and was determined to sieze them. Stephen moved north at the head of his royal army

but preferred to avoid a pitched battle with the Scottish forces because he knew that Matilda and Geoffrey were likely to invade England and he could not fight concurrent bloody wars on two fronts. Stephen and David found a peaceful compromise: the Scottish monarch obtained possession of Carlisle but had to renounce all the other frontier territories that he had captured during the previous weeks.

After obtaining this diplomatic success, Stephen held his first royal court at Easter, to which he invited most of the Anglo-Norman nobles. Many aristocrats and officials of the Church gathered at Westminster, where the king issued a new royal charter that confirmed all the promises already made to the Church. Stephen also promised to cancel all the royal abuses that had become increasingly common during the last years of Henry I's reign. Numerous grants of land and favours were given out by the king to the aristocrats who were present at the Easter court, and he also endowed numerous church foundations by giving further lands to the clergy. Stephen could count on the support of Louis VI, King of France, who was a personal enemy of Geoffrey of Anjou and would do anything in his power to avoid the formation of an Angevin Empire stretching across the English Channel. Consequently, by the end of 1136, Stephen's succession to the English throne was recognized as legitimate by Louis VI, as well as by Pope Innocent II, who was impressed by the many privileges conceded to the Church by the new monarch.

During 1136, Stephen experienced serious trouble in Wales, where his military position was not particularly stable. At the time of William the Conqueror's arrival in England, Wales had still been divided into a series of princedoms that were dominated by local warlords. These small states had a very aggressive attitude towards England, frequently launching violent incursions against the bordering English lands. William never attempted to annex Wales to his new dominions, instead simply adopting a defensive strategy in order to stop the incursions of the Welsh warriors. This policy

Opposite: The magnificent enamel effigy from the tomb of Geoffrey Plantagenet in Le Mans. Geoffrey V (1113–1151), Count of Anjou and Duke of Normandy, is considered as the real founder of the Plantagenet dynasty; by marrying Empress Matilda, in fact, he became a protagonist of the English political scene. His nickname of 'Plante Genest' or 'Planter of Broom' later started to identify the royal family initiated by his son Henry II. Since the Plantagenets' heartland was in Anjou, they were usually referred to as 'Angevins' in the contemporary sources. The funerary plaque showed in this photo, commissioned by Empress Matilda, is one of the earliest examples of Medieval heraldry; on the kite shield of Geoffrey, in fact, it is possible to see six golden rampant lions placed in three horizontal rows (with three, two and one figure from top to bottom) over a medium blue background. This motif was granted to a young Geoffrey by Henry I of England in 1128, according to the chronicler Jean de Marmentier; it was later adopted by Geoffrey's grandson William Longespée and probably gave origin to the three golden lions of the Royal Arms of England. Geoffrey is depicted wearing a richly ornamented emerald green tunic and a light blue cloak; the Phrygian headgear, quite popular in northern France, has an embroidered golden lion.

Knight with falchion sword
and axe. (*Photo and copyright
by Confraternita del Leone/
Historia Viva*)

Knight with mask helmet and kite shield. (*Photo and copyright by Confraternita del Leone/Historia Viva*)

was based on the creation of a series of earldoms in the border areas, possession of which was given to the most warlike Norman nobles. These earldoms became known as the Welsh Marches, working as a 'buffer zone' between England and Wales. The Norman warlords of the Welsh Marches were given special powers by William and could count on significant military forces. They did not limit themselves to a static defence of their territories, but gradually started to penetrate into the south-eastern territories of Wales. During Henry I's reign, several Norman castles were built in the border areas of Wales, but due to the resistance of the local population the English penetration in the region was never stable. Following Henry I's death, the Welsh launched renewed attacks against English territories and several minor revolts broke out in those portions of Wales that were under English control.

During early January 1136, Welsh forces gained a clear victory over the English at the Battle of Llwchwr, during which around 500 of Stephen's men were killed. The Welsh, like David I of Scotland, wanted to use the complicated political situation of England to their advantage and hoped to expel the foreign invaders from their borders. Most of the Welsh princes and warlords temporarily put aside their internal rivalries and joined forces to pursue a common goal. A Welsh army of some 6,000 men was thus assembled, including 2,000 cavalry equipped with chainmail like their Norman opponents, and won another great victory against the local English forces at the Battle of Crug Mawr, even burning the town of Cardigan (which was one of the main English military bases in Wales). After these unexpected setbacks, Stephen abandoned any hope of putting down the rebellion in Wales by the end of 1137, having instead to focus on the defence of his English and Norman possessions from attacks by Geoffrey of Anjou.

Geoffrey had started his offensive against the Duchy of Normandy during the early months of 1136, raiding and burning on an extensive scale rather than attempting a permanent occupation of Norman lands. In 1137, Stephen went to Normandy and held a crucial meeting with his older brother, Theobald (who was now the Count of Blois), and King Louis VI of France. They both supported Stephen and encouraged him to take the initiative against the Angevins. The English king, however, soon revealed all his military deficiencies. He had been forced to recruit a large contingent of Flemish mercenaries in order to field a significant army in France, but was not able to keep order among the ranks of his troops. Frictions between his Norman feudal contingents and the Flemish mercenaries soon transformed into violent clashes that led to the desertion of most of the Normans. Stephen thus had no choice but to agree a truce with Geoffrey, promising to pay him 2,000 marks a year in exchange for peace on the borders of Normandy. The military events that had taken place in Wales and France during 1137 had shown the martial limits of the new English king.

To make matters worse for the king, Robert of Gloucester, an illegitimate son of Henry I as well as one of the most powerful Anglo-Norman nobles, rose up in revolt against Stephen in 1138, initiating a long series of civil wars in England. Robert declared his support for Matilda and organized a regional rebellion in Kent from his personal dominions in France. Soon after these events, Geoffrey of Anjou renewed his attacks against southern Normandy and David I of Scotland invaded northern England again, aiming to penetrate as far south as Yorkshire. The Scottish monarch, having previously recognized the succession of Stephen as legitimate, changed sides and started to support Matilda. Stephen, facing a very complex military situation, decided to concentrate all his efforts in England: he sent his wife to Kent with an expedition from Boulogne in order to reconquer the key port of Dover, meanwhile moving some of his best knights to northern England in order to slow down the advance of David. In the northern territories, the English resistance was guided by Thurstan, the Archbishop of York. He was able to assemble an army of some 10,000 men, who stopped and defeated the 16,000 Scottish invaders at the Battle of the Standard. This blocked David's penetration into Yorkshire, but left most of Cumberland and Northumbria under Scottish control. Meanwhile, Stephen went to Wales in order to re-establish his defences in the Welsh Marches. He obtained some minor local successes, but could not inflict a resounding defeat on the Welsh princes. During the closing months of 1138, Matilda of Boulogne was able to recapture Dover and find a temporary agreement with the Scottish king (formalized in the Treaty of Durham): David remained in control of Carlisle and Cumberland, while his son and heir, Henry, was given Northumberland as a vassal of Stephen. The English king retained possession of the strategically important castles of Bamburgh and Newcastle, but had renounced a large portion of northern England in order to stabilize his political position. The Treaty of Durham led to two decades of peace on the Anglo-Scottish border, but caused great malcontent among the powerful Norman nobles of northern England, who had hoped that Stephen would defeat David I and retake all the lost territories. One of these nobles was Ranulf, Earl of Chester, who considered Carlisle and Cumberland as part of his personal dominions. Displeased by the conduct of his king, Ranulf gradually reduced his support for Stephen's cause.

By the beginning of 1139, an invasion of England by Matilda and Geoffrey seemed imminent. The pair had been able to occupy most of Normandy during the previous months, mobilizing substantial military forces with Robert. Stephen knew that the only way to retain control over his realm was to form a strong political alliance with the most important nobles, who in the event of an invasion would provide most of the king's troops; their loyalty was thus a vital factor in the ongoing dynastic struggle. Stephen created a large number of new earldoms, the possession of which was given to those nobles who were willing to support him in the civil war. Most of the new earls were experienced military commanders, who were deployed in the most vulnerable parts of England and were given additional powers by the king. Their main task,

Knight with full chainmail. (*Photo and copyright by Raven Verstad of Sirotci*)

Knight with spear and kite shield. (*Photo and copyright by "Confraternita del Leone/ Historia Viva*)

after the landing of Matilda's troops, was to put up a first line of defence against the invaders and to raise substantial military contingents for Stephen. The king also removed several bishops who were favourable to Matilda and had large territorial possessions. This caused several incidents, with some of the bishops trying to resist and damaging Stephen's relationship with a section of the English clergy. In August 1139, the invasion by Matilda and Geoffrey finally materialized. Baldwin de Revers, one of Matilda's best military commanders, crossed the English Channel and landed at Wareham in Dorset with the objective of capturing a major port where the bulk of Geoffrey's troops could disembark. Stephen's forces, however, were able to contain the moves of Baldwin de Revers, who was unable to occupy a substantial port.

On 30 September, Matilda and Robert of Gloucester landed at Arundel in Sussex with a small contingent of just 140 knights. The local castle became their main base, where Matilda installed a provisional court. Robert quickly moved north-west to reach Wallingford and Bristol, intending to raise popular support for Matilda as well as to link up with rebels who operated around Gloucester. Stephen's response to these moves was rapid: he marched south and besieged the castle of Arundel, trapping Matilda inside its walls. At this point, thanks to the mediation of Henry of Blois, a temporary truce was signed between the two warring factions. Matilda was released from the siege at Arundel and was allowed to unite her forces with those of Robert of Gloucester. There were two main reasons behind Stephen's decision to set Matilda free: first, he had no possibility of swiftly taking Arundel Castle, and a long siege would have only damaged his cause; and second, the main military threat to the stability of his rule was represented by Robert of Gloucester and not by Matilda (who had only a few knights with her at Arundel).

The following months proved positive for Matilda's cause, with her ally Robert able to expand his control over a vast area of England that stretched from Gloucester to Cornwall and from the Welsh Marches to Oxford. Matilda established a new provisional court in Gloucester, not far from the main stronghold of Robert at Bristol. In this phase of the civil war, Stephen tried to protect the city of London from attack by besieging the important castle of Wallingford in order to obtain control over the 'Thames Corridor'. This fortification, however, was well defended, and the king was unable to take it. Part of the royal army was left at Wallingford to blockade the garrison in the castle, while Stephen and the majority of his troops attacked various other minor castles in the Wiltshire area. The king's incursions, however, did not last for long, an enemy attack against his troops at Wallingford obliging him to return in order to defend London. The following months of stalemate proved very costly for the king: he did not have the economic resources to conduct a lengthy conflict, and several of his leading nobles were ready to abandon him at the first opportunity. Indeed, in early 1140, Nigel, Bishop of Ely, rebelled against Stephen in retaliation for

Knight with mask helmet and sword. (*Photo and copyright by Confraternita del Leone/Historia Viva*)

Knight with spear and helmet with nasal. (*Photo and copyright by Confraternita del Leone/Historia Viva*)

the confiscations that he had suffered during the previous year. The king responded rapidly to this new threat before Nigel could join forces with Robert of Gloucester. The bishop's main base was on the Isle of Ely, which was surrounded by protective fenland, but Stephen took his army into the fens and built a temporary bridge made of boats lashed together that allowed him to launch a surprise assault on the island. Nigel was utterly defeated but was able to escape alive.

While these events took place in eastern England, the military situation started to change also along the northern borders of the kingdom. Here, Ranulf of Chester decided to move against Prince Henry of Scotland in order to gain control over a vast portion of northern England. Prince Henry was by now one of Stephen's strongest supporters, realizing that in the event of Matilda's victory he would lose all the English lands that were under his control, having been given to him by the king. Ranulf first tried to kill Prince Henry by organizing an ambush, and when this proved unsuccessful he launched a surprise attack against the castle at Lincoln, which was held by Stephen's men. The king marched north with his troops, but instead of fighting against the rebel noble he agreed to a truce with him. Ranulf was allowed to retain control over the castle at Lincoln in exchange for siding with Stephen in the civil war. The truce, however, did not last long, for as soon as the royal army left northern England, Ranulf proclaimed his support for Matilda. At this point Stephen gathered his forces again and marched north in order to place Lincoln Castle under siege. Then in early 1141, while the king was with his troops around Lincoln, Robert of Gloucester joined forces with Ranulf of Chester and marched against Stephen with the objective of fighting a major pitched battle. The king held a council to decide whether to face the enemy or to wait for the arrival of reinforcements. In the end, Stephen decided to fight. The ensuing Battle of Lincoln, like most of the battles of Plantagenet England, was an affair between two small groups of heavily equipped knights: Stephen had 1,250 combatants (mostly experienced knights), while Robert of Gloucester and Ranulf of Chester had gathered around 1,000 men (a portion of whom were Welsh warriors). As soon as the battle began, most of the royalist nobles abandoned their king with their knights and switched sides. Robert of Gloucester then launched a frontal cavalry charge and Stephen was captured. The Battle of Lincoln proved a disaster for the king, who was thereafter imprisoned in Bristol.

Matilda, now able to take all necessary steps to have herself crowned, thus made a deal with Henry of Blois, who agreed to abandon his brother Stephen in exchange for receiving complete control over the clergy of England once Matilda was on the throne. A good portion of the aristocracy and the most important men of the Church were now favourable to Matilda, but the same could not be said for the population of London. Indeed, the future queen was generally perceived as a 'stranger' because of her husband. When Matilda advanced on London to stage her coronation in June 1141, the city rose

Knight with axe and
helmet with nasal.
(*Photo and copyright
by Confraternita del
Leone/Historia Viva*)

Knight with hauberk chainmail and sword. (*Photo and copyright by Confraternita del Leone/ Historia Viva*)

up in revolt. She was obliged to flee after being taken by surprise, and made a chaotic retreat to Oxford. While these events took place in England, Geoffrey of Anjou had continued fighting in France to complete his conquest of Normandy. The Duchy was almost defenceless because the political situation of France had changed dramatically. Theobald, Stephen's powerful brother, could no longer intervene to defend Normandy since he had to defend his own territories from the expansionism of the new French monarch, Louis VII. Geoffrey's successes in the Duchy, however, were perceived as a dangerous threat by many Anglo-Norman nobles who owned lands in England as well as Normandy. With Matilda's victory, they would have lost their French territories forever, since the new queen would have granted the lands to her husband Geoffrey. As a result, although the king had been taken captive, his cause remained alive. Matilda of Boulogne, Stephen's wife, played a crucial role in this phase of the civil war. She gathered all the forces that were still loyal to the king and marched to London, where the population was favourable to the royalist cause. After the rebellion in London, Henry of Blois decided to terminate his collaboration with Matilda and changed sides once again. He met with Matilda of Boulogne and transferred his support to her. Following their retreat from London, Robert of Gloucester and Matilda decided to attack Henry of Blois once he expressed his loyalty towards Stephen. Henry's episcopal castle of Winchester was besieged, but the besiegers were soon surrounded by troops assembled by Matilda of Boulogne. The besiegers then divided their forces into two: one, under the orders of Matilda, left the siege and fled, while the other, commanded by Robert, remained to fight but was completely defeated by the royalist army. During what became known as the 'Rout of Winchester', Robert was captured.

During November 1141, the two warring sides exchanged their military leaders: Stephen returned to London, while Robert joined Matilda in Oxford. With his brother's support, Stephen was crowned again at Christmas with his wife Matilda of Boulogne. During the early months of 1142, after a period of illness, Stephen travelled to northern England and met with the turbulent Ranulf of Chester. After complex negotiations, Ranulf was finally convinced to join the king and changed side once more. The summer of 1142 saw Stephen besieging newly built enemy castles such as those at Cirencester, Bampton and Wareham. Meanwhile, Robert of Gloucester had left England and gone to France with part of his military forces in order to assist Geoffrey in his operations in Normandy. Robert was sure that Matilda would have been able to retain Oxford while he was away, since the city was protected by strong walls and the Isis River. Contrary to all expectations, however, Stephen launched a swift attack against Oxford by swimming with part of his troops across the Isis. The attack was a success and the city was rapidly taken. Matilda was trapped in the castle and risked being captured. The fortress at Oxford, however, was very strong and Stephen was in no position to mount an assault against it. The king, rather than storming the castle, settled down for a long siege in a bid to capture Matilda. Against all odds, however, she was able to escape from the siege just before Christmas without being intercepted by royal troops. The following day, the garrison of the castle surrendered, but Stephen had not achieved his main objective of capturing Matilda.

After obtaining a series of victories in France, Robert of Gloucester returned to England at the head of a substantial number of men and immediately took the initiative. He attacked the castle of Wilton, which was an important base of the royalist troops in Herefordshire. Stephen was besieged in Wilton and had no choice but to fight a pitched battle against his enemies. He tried to move out from the castle, but was halted by a frontal cavalry charge led by Robert. The king was on the verge of being captured for a second time, but was able to flee from the battlefield. The Battle of Wilton, although a defeat for the royalists, was not a decisive one. During late 1143, Stephen faced a new military threat with a rebellion by the Earl of Essex, who had been obliged by the king to give up many of his fortifications around London over recent years, including the Tower of London. Sensing the right moment had come, the Earl of Essex rebelled against the king and launched a campaign from the Isle of Ely, where he had his main base. Stephen did not have the resources to crush Essex, but was able to limit the incursions he launched against London.

If the situation of Matilda's cause in England was at this time precarious, the same could not be said in France, where her husband Geoffrey had taken the important city of Rouen and been recognized as the Duke of Normandy. However, in September 1144, the Earl of Essex died during a raid on Burwell and his rebellion came to a sudden end. During 1145, the conflict continued with several victories for the king, who recaptured the castle of Faringdon in Oxfordshire and also captured Ranulf of Chester. Ranulf had to hand over several of his most important castles in order to avoid execution: as a result, Stephen regained control over the important fortifications of Lincoln and Coventry. Ranulf rebelled again as soon as he was relieved from captivity, and the political situation in northern England remained unstable during the following years. In 1147, Robert of Gloucester died from natural causes and Matilda decided to abandon England. Consequently, military operations lost much of their intensity and many nobles of the opposing factions started to make individual peace agreements between themselves. After Matilda's return to Normandy, her young son Henry landed in England at the head of a small mercenary contingent, but his expedition was rapidly defeated. In 1149, Henry returned to England, this time with the intention of forming an alliance with Ranulf of Chester and organizing an attack against the city of York. Stephen responded by rapidly marching north to face this new menace and prevented his enemies from investing York. Defeated without fighting for a second time, the young Henry returned to Normandy.

The son of Matilda and Geoffrey was made Duke of Normandy soon after these events, Henry thereafter starting to be seen by many as the best possible heir to the

Knight with mask helmet and kite shield. (*Photo and copyright by Confraternita del Leone/Historia Viva*)

throne of England. In 1152 he married Eleanor, Duchess of Aquitaine, who had recently divorced from Louis VII of France and controlled very large territorial domains. This union made Henry the future ruler of a huge portion of France and one of the most powerful aristocrats in Europe. Stephen, after many years of battles, was growing older and starting to plan the succession to his throne. His eldest son, Eustace, had already been given the County of Boulogne in 1147, and Stephen wanted to crown him in Westminster while he himself was still alive. In 1152, at Easter, the king gathered the English nobles in order to have them swear fealty to Eustace and asked the bishops of his realm to crown his eldest son as successor to the throne of England. The clergy, however, did not support Eustace's rise to power and the bishops opposed Stephen's plans. In 1153, Henry returned to England for a third time, again at the head of a small army. He proceeded to besiege the castle of Malmesbury but avoided a pitched battle against the king when Stephen tried to intercept him along the River Avon. Although Henry did not achieve any significant military success, an increasing number of nobles started to join his cause. Stephen tried to restore order among his barons by besieging the important

Knight with mace and helmet with nasal. (*Photo and copyright by Confraternita del Leone/Historia Viva*)

castle of Wallingford, which had fallen into rebel hands. However, the royalist siege failed when Henry marched against the king at the head of a small army. The two sides confronted each other across the River Thames at Wallingford, but no battle took place as the nobles of both sides had no intention of fighting. A truce was brokered and a private meeting took place between Stephen and Henry; to many contemporary observers, it seemed that the old king was now ready to cede his throne to Matilda's son. A few months after these events, Eustace died, thereby removing the most important claimant to the English throne. His demise was an important step towards a lasting pacification of the realm. Yet hostilities continued for some time, with Henry capturing Oxford as well as Stamford. Henry of Blois and Archbishop Theobald of Canterbury, however, were by now working to broker a permanent peace settlement to bring an end to the internecine warfare. A further meeting between Stephen and Henry resulted in the Treaty of Winchester being signed and the long civil war finally came to an end in 1153. Under its terms, Stephen adopted Henry as his son and successor, in return for Henry paying formal homage to him. The king's remaining son, William, renounced his claims to the English throne and recognized Henry as the future monarch. Stephen and Henry sealed the treaty with a famous 'kiss of peace' in Winchester Cathedral. Then on 25 October 1154, just a few months after putting an end to the civil war, Stephen died. Henry was subsequently crowned King of England and the new Plantagenet dynasty took control over the realm.

Henry II, son of Matilda and Geoffrey, was the first Plantagenet King of England, but at the time of his accession to the throne the royal family to which he belonged was still simply known as the Angevins. The monarchs who followed Henry II (starting with his sons Richard the Lionheart and John Lackland) are usually referred to as Angevin kings in contemporary English primary sources. It was only with Richard of York, in the fifteenth century, that the English royal family adopted the new denomination of Plantagenet, which was applied retroactively to all the English kings who came after Stephen. Nevertheless, the first three exponents of the new dynasty are still commonly known as Angevin kings because they had important political interests and territorial possessions in France, and thus were still strongly linked to their home region of Anjou. Their successors were, however, definitely more 'English' in their outlook. The term Plantagenet, introduced by Richard of York, derived from the French nickname *Plante Genest* that was attributed to Geoffrey of Anjou. *Genest* was the French version of the Latin word *Genista*, which was used to indicate the flowering plant that we know as Scotch Broom. The nickname *Plante Genest* actually meant 'the man who plants a Scotch Broom'. We don't know if Geoffrey of Anjou really had a passion for this plant, but whatever the case, Richard of York decided to create a new name for his family from the nickname of his ancestor.

Knight with falchion sword and kite shield. (*Photo and copyright by Confraternita del Leone/Historia Viva*)

Knight with mace and sword. (*Photo and copyright by Confraternita del Leone/Historia Viva*)

Chapter 2

The Reign of Henry II

After Stephen of Blois' sudden death, Henry II took oaths of loyalty from some of the most important English aristocrats. These men are usually referred to as 'barons' in the medieval sources, and thus we will use this term to indicate these warlike nobles of the realm. On 19 December 1154, Henry II was crowned at Westminster Abbey together with his wife, Eleanor of Aquitaine. The first royal court was gathered in April of the following year, which was the occasion for the new king to receive the formal submission of a large number of nobles. Henry's political position was quite stable from the outset, there being no potential rivals from a dynastic point of view except for Stephen's son, William, who died early during his reign. The new monarch, however, had inherited a devastated kingdom that had suffered greatly during the last decades of civil war. Unauthorized castles had been built by many aristocrats in various parts of the country, brigandage was widespread in some regions and the rights of the crown over common lands and forests were no longer respected by most of the population. The period known as The Anarchy had caused serious damage to the institutional structure created by William the Conqueror: even royal control over the coin mints had become limited, and this had important consequences for the financial capabilities of the crown. Henry II ordered the demolition of many unauthorized castles, tried to restore the system of royal justice and attempted to reorganize the royal finances by collecting taxes in a more effective way. All these measures, however, were carried out from a distance by the king, who spent six of his first eight years on the throne in France rather than in England. The new monarch faced serious political troubles on the continent, but also along the borders of England. As we have seen in the previous chapter, both the King of Scotland and the Welsh warlords had taken advantage of the English political struggles to enlarge their territorial possessions. Henry II, who can be seen as a true 'warrior king', soon tried to change the situation by limiting the ambitions of his rivals in the British Isles. In 1157, after having threatened to attack Scotland, Henry obtained from the new king north of the border (the young Malcolm IV, grandson of David I) the return of all the lands of northern England that had been taken by Scottish forces during the English civil war. In Wales, meanwhile, Henry conducted two military campaigns: one in the north (1157) and one in the south (1158). These resulted in the restoration of the *status quo* in the Welsh Marches, but did not see the occupation of any new territory by the English.

Henry II experienced the most serious of his military problems in France, where he had a very difficult relationship with Louis VII. The French king feared that the Angevin Empire could be a serious obstacle for the creation of a centralized monarchy in France, and saw Henry II as a great rival. In his early life, Henry had already clashed with Louis VII, who did not want to recognize him as the legitimate Duke of Normandy. This situation only worsened when Henry married Eleanor of Aquitaine, who had previously been Louis VII's wife and who controlled great swathes of French territory. Henry II created a strong network of alliances with some of the most important French nobles in order to secure his dominion over Normandy and Anjou; in addition to marrying Eleanor of Aquitaine, he concluded military alliances with the Count of Flanders and the Count of Blois. From a military point of view, Henry was much stronger than Louis. Consequently, Louis never tried to fight a full-scale war against the English king. For many years, however, France lived in a state of constant tension, with the borders of the Angevin Empire being frequently raided by nobles who were allied with Louis VII against Henry II. In 1154, soon after being crowned in Westminster, the new English king returned to France and concluded a peace treaty with Louis. He returned some territories to the French monarch but did not pay homage to him as a vassal of the French crown. In 1158, after years of growing tension between the two kings, Henry II's eldest son (who would die a few years later) married Louis VII's daughter, Margaret. Yet even this union did not lead to a thaw in the 'cold war' between Henry and Louis.

Henry II had a clear political plan in mind: he wanted to expand his territorial possessions in France as much as possible without fighting long wars. One of his primary targets was the Duchy of Brittany, located to the west of Normandy. The region was largely independent from the crown of France and had its own peculiar culture: Brittany, in fact, had long been inhabited by Celtic communities that had a lot in common with the Welsh and had been annexed to France only by Charlemagne (after some very costly military campaigns conducted by the Franks). The Bretons had their own language and traditions, which were very different from those of mainland France. Like Wales, Brittany was divided into a series of small princedoms whose warlike rulers were never fully submitted to the central authority of their duke. In 1148, Conan III, Duke of Brittany, died and a civil war broke out in the region. Henry II claimed to be the overlord of Brittany, since the duchy had owed loyalty to his predecessor Henry I some decades before. As a result, Henry supported one of the two sides fighting in Brittany so that the new duke would be favourable towards him. However, the pretender supported by Henry II (the future Conan IV) later changed

Knight with chainmail and great helm, a flat-topped cylinder that covered the head with only small openings for ventilation and vision. (*Photo and copyright by Raven Verstad of Sirotci*)

Knight with padded gambeson jacket and axe. (*Photo and copyright by Confraternita del Leone/Historia Viva*)

his political line and started to fight to preserve the autonomy of his homeland. As a result, Henry also changed his strategy and occupied the County of Nantes (located in the east of Brittany) in 1158. Louis VII of France did not intervene in the civil conflict of Brittany, at least not directly, since the region was part of the Angevins' sphere of political influence. Henry II did not operate only in northern France, but also in the south, where he aimed to enlarge his wife's possessions in Aquitaine. During the previous years, the important city of Toulouse, which had always been part of the Duchy of Aquitaine, had started to be ruled as an independent county. Henry would not accept such an act and thus concluded an alliance with the main enemy of Toulouse: Raymond Berenguer of Barcelona. The Count of Toulouse, Raymond V, tried to preserve the independence of his territories by forming an alliance with Louis VII of France: he married the latter's sister, Constance, in the hope of stopping Henry II's expansionism. The English king, however, attacked Toulouse and ravaged the countryside of the city before seizing various local castles and annexing the area of Quercy to Aquitaine. Once again, Henry II and Louis VII did not fight against each other on the battlefield, but the tensions between the two monarchs continued to grow.

After Henry also started to show his belligerency in Aquitaine, Louis VII decided to reinforce his political position by forming new alliances with important French aristocrats. After the death of his wife, he married the sister of the Counts of Blois and Champagne. These were extremely powerful nobles and controlled two of France's richest regions. The County of Blois was ruled by Theobald V and the County of Champagne by Henry I; the former had previously been an ally of Henry II but was becoming increasingly worried about the expansionist ambitions of the Angevins. When Theobald mobilized his forces along the border with Henry's French possessions, the English king responded by attacking the territory of Blois and conquering his rival's main castle after a ferociously contested siege. At the beginning of 1161, a full-blown war between Henry II and Louis VII seemed inevitable, but during the following year a peace treaty was worked out between the two kings thanks to the mediation of Pope Alexander III. This simply 'officialized' the situation existing on the ground and thus could be considered as a personal victory for Henry. He had been able to expand and stabilize the Angevin Empire without fighting a large-scale war. Yet Henry II's dominions did not have a coherent organization and were not under the control of a single government. Instead, they consisted of a loose and highly flexible network of feudal connections that were all linked to the Angevin family. Henry travelled widely across his empire, confirming his direct or indirect control over its various components and reforming the local governments in order to make them more efficient. Henry could count on the support of an emerging class

Knight with helmet with nasal and padded gambeson. (*Photo and copyright by Confraternita del Leone/Historia Viva*)

Knight with padded gambeson. (*Photo and copyright by Raven Verstad of Sirotci*)

of 'new men', minor aristocrats who were capable administrators and who rose to positions of prominence thanks to their personal loyalty towards the monarch. It was thanks to them that the Angevin Empire was kept together by Henry II, despite the opposition of some barons.

From 1164, Louis VII of France started to enlarge his anti-Angevin coalition by forming an alliance with the Duchy of Burgundy as well as with the new Count of Flanders, who unlike his predecessor was concerned about Henry II's expansionist policies and thus preferred to side with the King of France. The following year, Louis finally sired a male heir, the future Philip Augustus, thereby securing his own position as King of France against any future claim over his throne coming from the Angevins. Meanwhile Henry II had started to exert a more direct control over Brittany, launching a large-scale invasion of the region in 1166. The English king forced Conan IV to abdicate as duke and gave Brittany to Conan's daughter, Constance, who was betrothed to Henry II's son, Geoffrey. With this move, the English king showed his firm intention to include Brittany among the territories of the Angevin Empire. Henry also continued to act in other areas of France, most importantly in Aquitaine, where he prolonged his struggle with Raymond of Toulouse. He could now count on the support of the Archbishop of Bordeaux as well as of Alfonso II of Aragon, and consequently, Raymond was forced to divorce from Louis VII's sister and came under the political influence of Henry II. In 1167, after these events, open war finally broke out between the Angevin monarch and the King of France. Louis VII allied himself with the Kingdom of Scotland, the Welsh princedoms and the Bretons in the hope of crushing the empire of his rival. Normandy was attacked by French troops, but Henry responded with a violent counter-attack that destroyed the main logistical base of his enemy at Chaumont-sur-Epte. After this defeat, before the war could be enlarged, Louis VII abandoned his allies and made a truce with the English king. Henry was then free to crush the Bretons and restore his rule over their duchy. During subsequent years, the English monarch, becoming increasingly concerned about the succession to his throne, decided that his empire would be divided into three parts after his death: his first son, Henry, would receive England and Normandy, while Richard would be given the Duchy of Aquitaine and Geoffrey would receive the Duchy of Brittany. In 1169, the king met with his old rival Louis VII at Montmirail, where the French monarch recognized Henry's plans for the division of his domains as legitimate, in exchange for receiving formal homage from Henry's sons. The years following the peace agreement of Montmirail saw Henry II reinforcing his position in southern France, concluding alliances with the Count of Savoy in the east and the King of Castile in the west. The daughter of the Count of Savoy was promised to Henry's son, John, while the King of Castille married Henry's daughter, Eleanor. Thanks to these intelligent diplomatic moves, the King of England finally obtained the submission of Raymond of Toulouse in 1173, with the city once again coming under the influence of Aquitaine.

As is clear from the events outlined above, Henry II spent most of his life as a king dealing with French political questions, passing only a limited amount of time in England. Nevertheless, he is still very well known in Britain, largely due to the controversial events that led to the assassination of Thomas Becket. When the Archbishop of Canterbury, Theobald of Bec, died in 1161, Henry saw an opportunity to reassert his royal rights over the Church in England. As we have seen, the reign of Stephen had been a very positive period for a large portion of the English clergy, which had been given many privileges in exchange for supporting Stephen's rise and permanence on the throne. Henry II chose Thomas Becket, his old friend and chancellor, as the new Archbishop of Canterbury. The monarch believed that Becket would remain extremely loyal to him, but his plans did not work as expected. Indeed, Becket changed his political ideas soon after becoming archbishop and started to act as a fierce protector of the Church's rights in England. Becket tried to regain control over several lands that had been expropriated to the bishops by the royal government, and opposed Henry's new taxation policies. Another source of conflict between the archbishop and the king was the treatment meted out to members of the clergy who committed secular crimes. According to Henry II's view, these individuals had to be judged by the royal courts, like all the other subjects of the kingdom; yet according to Becket, they should be judged only by clerical courts.

In 1164, under strong pressure from the king, the Archbishop of Canterbury was forced to accept the promulgation of the Constitutions of Clarendon that gave Henry II a legal basis according to which members of the clergy could be judged by royal courts in the event of them having committed secular crimes. A few months after this, Thomas Becket fled to France, where he could count on the personal protection of Henry II's mortal enemy: Louis VII. Henry then started to persecute Becket's supporters, while the archbishop excommunicated all the religious and civil authorities who sided with the monarch. At that time, the papacy was experiencing a period of great troubles in Italy, with Holy Roman Emperor Frederick I fighting against the Italian cities and the Papal States in order to exert a more direct political control over the Italian peninsula. The Pope supported Becket in principle but was in no position to excommunicate the King of England since Henry could be an ally for him in his struggle with Frederick I. In 1169, Henry II decided to crown his first son, Henry, as King of England and thus needed to make peace – at least temporarily – with the Archbishop of Canterbury. Becket, however, refused any reconciliation with

Knight with sword and kite shield. (*Photo and copyright by Confraternita del Leone/Historia Viva*)

Knight with sword
and helmet with nasal.
(*Photo and copyright by
Confraternita del Leone/
Historia Viva*)

the king, so Henry II's son had to be crowned by the Archbishop of York. At this point the Pope authorized Becket to lay an interdict on England to apply pressure on the king. Under such an interdict, no inhabitants of England could receive the sacrament or be married, causing great malcontent among the populace. In order to find a solution to this new crisis, Henry II agreed to come to terms with Becket, who returned to England in December 1170. Once in the realm, however, the Archbishop of Canterbury excommunicated another three supporters of Henry II, causing the fury of the monarch. In response to this act, the king sent four of his knights to Canterbury with orders to arrest Becket for having broken his agreement with the crown. The archbishop resisted arrest inside his cathedral and was killed by the knights. This event, unprecedented in the history of Christian Europe, horrified the Pope and the clergy of England. Becket was declared a martyr soon after his death and became a symbol of the Church's resistance against the attacks of the monarchies. Louis VII used the episode to his advantage in order to present Henry II as a violent man without moral principles. Within a few months the international pressure on the King of England became so strong that Henry was forced to negotiate a settlement with the Pope in May 1172. According to this, Henry II would organize a crusade to free the Holy Land from the Muslims and would overturn the Constitutions of Clarendon. Although Henry never went to the Holy Land, he was able to restore his position in the eyes of the papacy without suffering any further damage.

During the second half of his reign, Henry II spent most of his energies in establishing some form of direct English control over Ireland. The three Norman kings and Stephen of Blois had never attempted to land on the island at the head of an army; they had plans to do so, especially William the Conqueror and Henry I, but their involvement on other fronts prevented them from taking action. By the time of Henry II's accession to the English throne, Ireland was controlled by a series of small kingdoms that were ruled by warlike princes. These were constantly at war against each other and could count – more or less – on similar military resources. The Kingdom of Leinster was the strongest of all, since it controlled a large portion of southern Ireland. It was on good terms with Henry II even before 1154, but always remained fully independent from England. The Irish Church was also completely autonomous from the English one, since it had not yet implemented the Gregorian Reforms that had been widely accepted in the rest of Europe. The Gaelic society of Ireland retained many pre-Christian features and feudalism had not yet been imported to the island from England. Consequently, the Irish princes and their subjects were very different from their English counterparts. However, the Archbishop of Canterbury had some claims to primacy over the Irish Church, and this was a strong factor behind Henry II's decision to invade Ireland. The English

Knight with spear and kite shield. (*Photo and copyright by Confraternita del Leone/Historia Viva*)

Knight with
great helm
and triangular
shield. (*Photo
and copyright by
Confraternita del
Leone/Historia
Viva*)

clergy wanted to impose the Gregorian Reforms over the population of Ireland, who were depicted as barbarian and semi-pagan by most contemporary English observers. The Anglo-Norman barons were also interested in the conquest of Ireland, since the occupation of new lands would give them new feudal possessions and titles.

In 1166, a coalition of Irish princedoms, led by the Kingdom of Connacht, attacked Leinster to oust the local ruler, Diarmait mac Murchada. Having been defeated, Diarmait left Ireland and sought help from his ally, Henry II. The English king, who had been waiting for an opportunity to intervene in Ireland, gave Diarmait permission to recruit an army on his lands. Several English barons, mostly from the Welsh Marches, agreed to help the deposed King of Leinster by landing in Ireland at the head of their troops. Among these there was Richard FitzGilbert de Clare, famous for his nickname of 'Strongbow'. Diarmait promised Strongbow his daughter in marriage and the future kingship of Leinster. In May 1169, the English allies of Diarmait landed in Ireland at Bannow Bay at the head of a small force that comprised forty knights, sixty men-at-arms and 360 archers. They were soon joined by 500 Irish warriors who had been recruited by the deposed ruler of Leinster. The combined Anglo-Irish force besieged the seaport of Wexford and reconquered the whole Kingdom of Leinster before defeating the forces of the neighbouring Kingdom of Ossory. Thereafter, the large coalition guided by Connacht that had deposed Diarmait was re-formed and moved against Leinster again. At this point, a peace agreement was agreed between the warring sides: Diarmait was acknowledged as the legitimate King of Leinster in exchange for agreeing to send his English allies away from Ireland. Shortly after making peace with his enemies, however, Diarmait was reinforced by a new English expeditionary force and marched north from Leinster to raid the countryside around Dublin. What had started as a simple English intervention in an Irish war was now becoming a full-scale invasion. In 1170, Strongbow landed in Ireland at Passage with 1,200 men, 200 of whom were heavily armoured knights. They assaulted Waterford and captured it after killing 700 Irish warriors. Diarmait then joined Strongbow at Waterford and the marriage between his daughter and the English warlord finally took place. Meanwhile, the Irish anti-Leinster coalition had been re-formed for a third time and was ready to intercept the Anglo-Irish forces of Strongbow and Diarmait. However, the pair bypassed the coalition forces by travelling over the Wicklow Mountains and reached Dublin. The city was then stormed and taken by surprise, an event that proved a turning point in the conflict since it marked the beginning of a 'total war' in Ireland. In May 1171, Diarmait died suddenly, after having obtained several other victories over his enemies. Consequently, Strongbow claimed the throne of Leinster for himself. According to Irish law, however, succession to kingship was elective and could only be passed on through the male line of a family, so the claims of the English warlord were rejected by members of Diarmait's extensive family. Only Diarmait's son, Domnall, backed Strongbow.

Soon after Diarmait's death, the Kingdom of Leinster joined the anti-English alliance, and Strongbow's army came under attack both from within Leinster and from outside the realm. Waterford was invested and Dublin also became a target of the Irish counter-offensive. A large Irish army, comprising contingents from every corner of the island, surrounded Dublin, operating in combination with a fleet of thirty warships that blockaded the city's bay. Part of the English garrison in Wexford went to Dublin to reinforce its defenders, but the Irish princes used this move to their advantage by launching a rapid attack against Wexford and taking it while the garrison was weakened. Dublin was besieged for two months. Several skirmishes took place, but the Irish force never attempted to assault the city since their plan was to starve it into surrender. Having lost Waterford and Wexford, and with Dublin under siege, Strongbow agreed to negotiate with his enemies. The peace talks, however, were used by the English only to gain some time, as they had no intention of renouncing all the territories that they had conquered in Ireland. Before the diplomatic moves were concluded, the English garrison of Dublin organized a successful surprise attack against the Irish camp. Hundreds of Irish warriors were killed and the siege of Dublin was practically broken. Following this defeat, the Irish troops withdrew from around Dublin. The English presence in Ireland had by now become quite strong, and the events around Dublin proved that it would be no easy task for the local princes to expel the invaders.

By this point of the war, Henry II feared that Strongbow may set up an independent kingdom in Ireland, which could dominate the commercial routes crossing the Irish Sea. The English invasion had essentially started as a private enterprise, organized in support of the Kingdom of Leinster, but now that the alliance between England and Leinster was no longer in existence, Henry wanted to use the footholds gained by Strongbow in order to conquer a large part of Ireland. In 1171, Henry ordered all his subjects fighting in Ireland to return home; if they refused to do so, all their possessions would be seized by the crown. Strongbow was left with no choice but to respond to the king's move by stating that all the conquests he had made were at the disposal of the monarch. Having brought Strongbow back under his control, Henry II made him the Royal Constable in Ireland and granted him most of the territories that he had taken in the previous years. In September 1171, the English king finally decided to organize a royal expedition to Ireland. He landed a few weeks later at Waterford with a large army that comprised 500 knights and 4,000 other soldiers. This was the first time a King of England had landed on Irish soil, an event that would have enormous importance for the history of the British Isles. The English

Knight with spear, mace and sword. (*Photo and copyright by Confraternita del Leone/Historia Viva*)

Knight with mask helmet, sword and triangular shield. (*Photo and copyright by Confraternita del Leone/ Historia Viva*)

troops marched to Dublin, where they joined forces with the local garrison, and Henry assumed formal control over all the Irish lands that were still in English hands. Dublin, Waterford and Wexford were made 'crown lands', while the Kingdom of Leinster was assigned to Strongbow, who was to rule it as a fiefdom of England. Many of these possessions still had to be reconquered, but Henry was sure of his final victory. The minor Irish princes, impressed by the military resources at the disposal of the English king, decided to submit without a fight in order to avoid an invasion of their realms. The King of Connacht, who also held the important honorific title of High King of Ireland, did not submit, and was joined by another two Irish monarchs.

The Irish Church submitted to King Henry, hoping that the arrival of the English would bring peace and political stability to their country. The English monarch organized a synod at Cashel, during which he was recognized by the bishops of Ireland as their temporal overlord. Henry was supported in this political and religious process by Pope Alexander III, who considered the submission of the Irish bishops to the English crown as the first step to imposing the Gregorian Reforms over the clergy of Ireland. Until that moment, unlike what happened in England, the Irish clergy had never paid to Rome the sums expected by the papacy; Irish society was not organized along the same feudal lines as the rest of Europe. With the early English conquests of Henry II, new monastic communities and military orders under the direct control of the papacy were introduced into Ireland. In April 1172, without having seen much action, Henry returned to England. He left behind some of the most warlike English nobles, including Hugh de Lacy, and most of his royal troops. In early 1173, however, most of the English barons operating in Ireland abandoned the island to fight for Henry II in the Great Revolt of 1173–1174.

With the departure of the king and the subsequent outbreak of another civil war in England, the remaining English barons in Ireland limited themselves to launching incursions against the Irish kingdoms that had not accepted Henry as their overlord. Dublin, Waterford and Wexford continued to be the main operational bases of the English, whose most important military leader remained Strongbow. In 1174, however, he suffered a significant defeat at the Battle of Thurles, which was won by the new High King of Ireland, Roderic O'Connor. Following this clash, realizing that the English military presence in Ireland had been greatly reduced, the Irish princes who had been submitted by the English rose up in revolt and joined the existing anti-Strongbow coalition. Dublin was besieged again, but luckily for the English a large relief expedition arrived before the Irish could secure victory. In 1175, following devastating raiding operations organized by the English, Henry II and the High King of Ireland decided to come to terms, signing the Treaty of Windsor. This divided Ireland into two spheres of influence: Henry continued to rule over

Battle of knights in a contemporary miniature.

the lands that had already been conquered, while the High King of Ireland obtained control over the rest of the island. Strongbow died in 1176, and the following year, English possessions in Ireland were organized as the Lordship of Ireland. According to Henry II's plans, these would be given to his son, John, when he latter came of

Knight with mask helmet, sword and triangular shield. (*Photo and copyright by Pisa Ghibellina*)

age. In the following years, the English nobles in Ireland again started to attack the Irish kingdoms of Desmond, Thomond and Connacht in attempts to expand the Lordship of Ireland. The Treaty of Windsor had proven very short-lived; Henry wanted to transform Ireland into a kingdom for John and intended to include this new realm in his ever-expanding empire.

While these events took place in Ireland, from 1173 onwards Henry II had to face the so-called Great Revolt, a civil war that almost destroyed the unity of the Angevin Empire and took place in several different areas of Europe. Henry II's first son, commonly known as Young Henry, had already been crowned as his father's successor but was very unhappy with his position. He played no role in the government of his future kingdom and was always kept short of money by his father. Geoffrey, Duke of Brittany, was also unhappy with his father's political decisions, as was Richard; the latter was strongly supported by his mother, Eleanor of Aquitaine, whose relationship with King Henry had by now completely disintegrated. Seeing that three of the king's sons and his wife were opposed to the policies carried out by the crown, many English barons decided to organize a revolt with the objective of deposing Henry II and replacing him with Young Henry. When the king gave to his youngest son, John, three important castles belonging to Young Henry, the latter left England and went to Paris under the protection of Louis VII. He was soon followed by his brothers Richard and Geoffrey. Eleanor also tried to go to Paris, but was captured by her husband's men before being able to do so. Young Henry could count on the support of Louis since he promised to cede several parts of his father's French possessions to the French nobles if they would support him against Henry II. The new King of Scotland, William, also supported Young Henry.

Within a few months, all the major barons of the Angevin Empire revolted against their king; only Normandy and Anjou remained loyal to Henry II. In May 1173, Louis VII and Young Henry attempted a pincer movement against Normandy, but this failed completely when Henry II mounted a devastating counter-offensive. Following this success, the royalist troops crushed the rebels of Brittany and brought the region back under the control of the English king. In the British Isles, the king was able to stop and defeat a Scottish invasion of northern England, but soon had to face a new menace when the Earl of Leicester, the leader of the revolting English barons, disembarked in Suffolk at the head of 3,000 Flemish mercenaries. This force, however, was crushed by a royal army at the Battle of Fornham, during which the Earl of Leicester and several other rebel nobles were captured. There was a second Scottish invasion of northern England in 1174, but that too ended in failure because the attackers were not able to occupy various strategic castles whose garrisons remained loyal to King Henry. Some months after these events, the Count of Flanders, who had joined the coalition led by Young Henry and Louis VII, sent a minor military force to East Anglia and started organizing a larger invasion of England. The king was forced to leave Normandy in order to defend England, but was able to expel the Flemish forces from his realm. Meanwhile, in France, Louis VII and his son, Philip, obtained several victories in Normandy and reached Rouen. After having restored the situation in England, however, Henry II returned to France and reconquered that portion of Normandy which had been lost. Understanding that the revolts in the Angevin Empire had all been crushed and that Normandy was impossible to conquer, Louis VII had no choice but to come to terms with Henry II. The King of England restored the *status quo*: Young Henry agreed to cede the disputed English castles to his brother, John (who had remained loyal to his father), but in exchange received two castles in Normandy. Richard and Geoffrey were granted half the revenues from Aquitaine and Brittany respectively. Eleanor of Aquitaine was kept under house arrest, since the king considered her as the mastermind of the Great Revolt. William of Scotland was forced to cede five important castles, while Philip of Flanders was obliged to assume a neutral position in the following years. By the end of 1174, Henry II was at the peak of his personal power, but his relationship with Louis VII of France remained very complicated.

In 1177, Henry II made John the Lord of Ireland, as planned some years before, and in 1179 he gave the Duchy of Aquitaine to Richard. Two years later, in 1181, Geoffrey finally became Duke of Brittany after marrying the daughter of his predecessor. Meanwhile, Young Henry spent his time travelling across Europe without playing a significant role in the government of his father. In 1182, having seen that John was the favourite of the king, he reiterated his previous demands that had caused the outbreak of the Great Revolt. Like his brothers, he wanted to be granted a portion of the Angevin Empire – notably the Duchy of Normandy – and wanted a sum of money to support himself with royal dignity. Henry II rejected these requests as he had done previously, but agreed to increase his eldest son's allowances. It became clear that tension was rising again in the Angevin Empire, so to placate his eldest son, Henry II asked Richard and Geoffrey to give homage to Young Henry for their lands. The heir to the English throne, however, refused to accept the formal submission of Richard due to personal reasons. He wanted to expel his brother from Aquitaine, and thus formed an alliance with some of the barons from the region who were unhappy with Richard's rule. Geoffrey sided with Young Henry and provided him with an army of Breton mercenaries. In 1183, open war broke out between Henry's sons: the king sided with Richard and fought with him in Aquitaine. After a few months, before either side could win a decisive battle, Young Henry caught a fever and died. Henry II consequently had to rearrange the plans for his succession

Knight with great
helm, sword and
triangular shield. (*Photo
and copyright by Pisa
Ghibellina*)

Knight with camail protecting the neck and shoulders and sword. (*Photo and copyright by Confraternita del Leone/Historia Viva*)

and redistribute the lands of the Angevin Empire among his surviving sons. Richard was to become the new King of England and Duke of Normandy, Geoffrey would retain Brittany and John would be given Aquitaine. Richard, however, refused to give up Aquitaine and disobeyed his father. At this point Geoffrey and John attacked the contested duchy on behalf of their father. Thus began a short war which ended in stalemate a few months later. During 1185, thanks to the intervention of Eleanor of

Aquitaine, Richard made peace with his father and finally handed over Aquitaine. In that same year, John organized an expedition against Ireland. It was not a great success, the English prince achieving little more than building several new castles. Then in 1186, Geoffrey died during a tournament, which once again changed Henry's plans for his succession.

In 1180, the King of France and mortal enemy of Henry II, Louis VII, had died, being replaced on the throne by his ambitious son, Philip Augustus. The new king was determined to destroy the Angevin Empire and was ready to use the frictions existing inside the English royal family to his advantage. In 1186, Philip asked Henry II for permission to have custody of Geoffrey's children and of the Duchy of Brittany; clearly, he wanted to expel the Angevins from the French fiefdom. If Henry rejected Philip's request, the French king said his forces would attack Normandy. No agreement was reached and both sides mobilized their troops, leading to an indecisive clash that took place before the intervention of the Pope who sponsored a truce. During the ensuing negotiations, the King of France tried to convince Richard to join his cause, but with little success. Henry II was still too strong to be defeated. Meanwhile, during 1187, the holy city of Jerusalem was conquered by Saladin and calls for a new crusade swept Europe. Richard was enthusiastic about the idea of organizing a crusade, but both Henry II and Philip of France had no intention of wasting their time with what they considered a futile military enterprise. Richard, as 'junior monarch' of England, started to raise taxes and to make plans for the expedition to the Holy Land, but his preparations were opposed by his father. Meanwhile, Richard also stabilized his position in Aquitaine, attacking the Count of Toulouse, who was a loyal ally of Philip. Richard's military initiative, which had not been authorized by his father, led to the outbreak of a new conflict between the Angevin Empire and France. Henry II wanted to avoid a large-scale war with Philip, and thus tried to convince the French king to agree to a long-term peace deal. The young French monarch rejected the offer and hostilities commenced, albeit with low intensity. By this time, the relationship between Henry II and Richard had finally dissolved, the son accusing the father of being against the crusade that he was organizing with great difficulty.

In 1188, Richard finally abandoned his father and joined King Philip, paying formal homage to him as Duke of Normandy. The papacy, having as its main objective the freeing of the Holy Land from the Muslims, then intervened again and a new peace conference was organized in 1189. By that time, Henry II was suffering from a severe bleeding ulcer and his health was deteriorating rapidly. The peace talks achieved very little, since the English monarch revealed his intention to cede his main possessions to John and not to Richard as agreed previously. After the diplomatic meetings ended, Philip and Richard launched a surprise attack against Henry II's forces in France.

Knight with mask helmet. (*Photo and copyright by Confraternita del Leone/Historia Viva*)

The King of England had no choice but to retreat to Normandy, where he prepared to face his enemies' offensive. During most of his life, the Angevin monarch had been a great military leader, and in this campaign – which would prove to be his last one – he showed all his capabilities. Instead of defending the borders of Normandy as expected by his opponents, he turned south towards Anjou to launch a counter-offensive. Here, however, his health worsened. Before he died, the king was visited by Richard. Father and son had a final meeting and some sort of reconciliation took

Battle of knights in a contemporary miniature.

place, with Richard once again designated as the future King of England. Shortly after, having been informed that John, his favourite son, had also sided with Richard and Philip, Henry II died in Chinon on 6 July 1189. He had been one of the greatest monarchs in the history of Medieval Europe.

Chapter 3

The Wars of Richard the Lionheart

Richard I, arguably the most famous monarch in the history of Medieval England, was officially invested as Duke of Normandy a few days after the death of his father, then on 3 September 1189, he was crowned King of England in Westminster Abbey. After spending just a few months in England to stabilize his political position, Richard soon resumed his military preparations for the long-awaited crusade. Reconquering Jerusalem had become an obsession for most of Europe's inhabitants, including the King of England. By fighting in the Holy Land, Richard hoped to gain glory for himself after having been overshadowed by his father for so long. Philip Augustus of France, who had been an ally of Richard during the last phase of Henry II's long reign, now feared that the new English king could become too popular in France due to his will to organize a new crusade. In 1188, Philip had officially promised to participate in the liberation of Jerusalem, so not doing so now would have had an extremely negative impact on his reputation as a pious monarch. After having analyzed the situation, Philip agreed to go on the Third Crusade, together with Richard. Frederick Redbeard, Holy Roman Emperor and enemy of the Church, also joined the kings of England and France in the venture. Richard, unlike Philip, was full of religious zeal, spending most his father's treasury and raising taxes to finance the crusade. He even agreed to free King William I of Scotland from his oath of loyalty to the King of England in exchange for a payment of 10,000 marks. To raise more funds, Richard sold rights to hold public positions and lands to anyone interested in them. Those royal officials who already had important roles in the administration had to pay large sums of money in order to retain their positions. Before leaving Europe, Richard replaced the local administrators of his French domains with new officials who were loyal to him and left part of his troops in France in order to protect his possessions from any attacks. In the summer of 1190, Richard the Lionheart finally set out on the crusade.

In September that year, Richard and Philip arrived in Sicily. The island was the most prosperous region of the Kingdom of Sicily, which had been founded in 1130 and comprised most of southern Italy. The Italian realm was governed by a Norman royal family, so its aristocracy had many links with the English nobility. In 1189, King William II of Sicily had died and southern Italy had seen the beginning of a civil war fought between two pretenders to the throne. On one side there was Tancred, cousin of the dead monarch, who seized power in Sicily thanks to the support of his warlike aristocracy; on the other was William II's aunt, Constance, wife of the new Holy Roman Emperor Henry VI (son of Frederick Redbeard, who had died on his way to the Holy Land) and legal heir to the Kingdom of Sicily. After taking power, Tancred had imprisoned William II's widow, Queen Joan, who was Richard's sister, and had refused to give her the money she had inherited according to William's will. When Richard landed in Sicily, where the port city of Messina was the main logistical base of the crusaders, he demanded the release of his sister and the immediate payment of her inheritance. On 28 September, Tancred released Joan but did not pay the sum that Richard was wanting. The presence of many English and French soldiers in Sicily added confusion to the political struggles that ravaged the kingdom. Indeed, the population of the island perceived the strangers as a potential menace and were jealous of their realm's independence. In October, the people of Messina rose up against the crusaders and demanded that the foreigners leave their land. Richard, in order to show his military superiority to both Tancred and Philip, who were near Messina, attacked the city and captured it on 4 October 1190. After looting and burning Messina, Richard transformed the Sicilian port into his main military base. On 4 March, after several months of increasing tension and thanks to the mediation of Philip, a treaty was signed between Richard and Tancred, according to which Joan was to receive 20,000 ounces of gold as compensation for her inheritance.

After these events, Richard and Philip remained in Sicily to complete their preparations before sailing to the Holy Land. During this period, however, tensions increased between the monarchs, despite them being allies (at least on paper). Frequent skirmishes took place between the English and French soldiers, while Philip started plotting with Tancred of Sicily against Richard. However, open hostilities were avoided and both monarchs left southern Italy in the spring of 1191. The crusader fleet of Richard was dispersed by a storm during its journey across the Mediterranean, and some of the king's ships, including those transporting his sister Joan and his promised wife, Berengaria of Navarre, were forced to dock in Cyprus. Once on the island, the two women were captured by the local ruler, Isaac Comnenos. In May, Richard arrived in Cyprus at the head of his forces, ordering Isaac to release his English prisoners and give his treasure to the crusaders. The ruler of Cyprus refused, and Richard took the important city of Limassol in retaliation. All the crusader leaders who were in Cyprus supported the Lionheart, as well as some local magnates who were against Isaac Comnenos. As a result, by the beginning of July, the King of England had been able to conquer the whole island of Cyprus and to capture Isaac. The occupation of Cyprus had a great strategic importance,

Knight with great helm and falchion sword. (*Photo and copyright by Pisa Ghibellina*)

Knight with great helm. (*Photo and copyright by Antichi Popoli*)

since its ports could now act as naval bases for the crusaders. After selling his newly conquered territories to the Knights Templar, Richard left Cyprus for Acre on 5 June. Before leaving Limassol, he married Berengaria, who was the heir of the Spanish Kingdom of Navarre, which bordered with the southern part of Aquitaine and thus was of great strategic importance for Richard.

On 9 October 1192, after more than a year spent fighting in the Holy Land, Richard the Lionheart decided to return to England. He had shown all his valour in the Kingdom of Jerusalem and had defeated the Muslims on several occasions, but he had not been able to change the political situation of the Levant as he had hoped. A fragile peace was concluded with Saladin and the most important questions remained unsettled. In the Holy Land, the Lionheart had to face the hostility of the other crusader leaders, who saw his participation in the Third Crusade as a threat to their expansionist ambitions in the Levant. The rivalry between Richard and Philip Augustus became even stronger in the Kingdom of Jerusalem, and would soon lead to the outbreak of renewed hostilities in Europe. The Lionheart's journey to England, however, did not go as planned: bad weather forced him to stop at Corfu, a Greek island that was part of the Byzantine Empire. The island was dominated by Emperor Isaac II Angelos, who was still furious with Richard for his occupation of Cyprus, which had long been a possession of the Byzantines. In order to avoid capture on Byzantine land, the King of England was forced to sail from Corfu disguised as a normal knight and with just four attendants. The ship transporting him, however, was wrecked near Aquileia in north-eastern Italy. At this point, Richard was forced to continue his journey by following a dangerous route that crossed the lands of central Europe dominated by the Holy Roman Empire.

Shortly before Christmas, not far from Vienna, Richard was captured by the men of Leopold of Austria. Leopold had participated in the Third Crusade with the Lionheart and had been one of its main leaders together with the monarchs of England and France. In the Kingdom of Jerusalem, Richard and Leopold had supported two different candidates to the local throne, and the King of England had humiliated the Archduke of Austria by casting down his standard from the walls of Acre. The imprisonment of Richard had no real legal basis and was the result of an arbitrary decision of Leopold, who was excommunicated by the Pope for his actions. In March 1193, the Lionheart was handed over to Henry VI, the Holy Roman Emperor, who imprisoned him in one of his castles. Henry was furious with the Lionheart because the English king had recognized Tancred as King of Sicily during his stay in southern Italy instead of supporting the claims of his wife, Constance. The Holy Roman Emperor was organizing a major military expedition to conquer the Kingdom of Sicily, for which he needed a lot of money: as a result, he decided to hold

Battle of knights in a contemporary miniature.

Knight with mask helmet and camail. (*Photo and copyright by Confraternita del Leone/Historia Viva*)

the King of England for ransom and demanded 150,000 marks for his liberation. This was a huge sum by the standards of the time, corresponding to two or three times the annual income of the English crown. Richard's mother, Eleanor of Aquitaine, soon started to work to raise the 150,000 marks, taxing both clergy and laymen for a quarter of the value of their properties. The treasures of the churches were confiscated and some extra money was raised from ordinary taxes. Before leaving England for the Holy Land, Richard had tried to secure for himself the loyalty of his brother, John, by giving him some of the richest English counties (Cornwall, Derby, Devon, Dorset, Nottingham and Somerset). During the Lionheart's absence, however, John started to act as though he was king, creating an independent royal court and beginning to nurture dangerous ambitions. First of all he wanted to replace William de Longchamp, who had been nominated as chancellor by his brother; secondly, he wanted to be recognized as the future monarch of England. After several weeks of growing tensions, armed conflict broke out between John and Longchamp. By October 1191, Longchamp had been defeated and John controlled most of the realm. John could count on the support of several nobles as well as the population of London, since he had made great promises to the inhabitants of the city. By that time Richard was already in Cyprus, but he was able to organize a counter-offensive against his brother from a distance, sending Walter of Coutances, the Archbishop of Rouen, to England with the task of restoring order.

A new phase of political turmoil began, during which John began exploring the possibility of concluding an alliance with Philip Augustus of France (who had returned from the crusade before Richard). After the Lionheart was captured in Austria, John began asserting that his brother was dead in order to be crowned as his heir. This attempt, however, failed in the face of opposition by those loyal to King Richard. John then went to Paris, where he finally allied himself with the King of France. John agreed to set aside his wife, Isabella of Gloucester, and to marry Philip's sister, Alys. Together, John and Philip offered 80,000 marks for Henry VI to hold Richard prisoner for several more years. The Holy Roman Emperor, however, turned down the offer, wanting to be paid the 150,000 marks he had demanded from the beginning. Finally, thanks to great efforts by Eleanor of Aquitaine, the ransom was paid, and Richard was freed on 4 February 1194. During the previous months, fighting had taken place in England between John's supporters and those of the king, but the royalist forces had few difficulties in keeping the situation under control. The famous stories of Robin Hood and Ivanhoe are set during this historical period, one of the most controversial of Plantagenet England. With the Lionheart's return to England, John's supporters surrendered and their leader retreated to Normandy. Richard did not punish his younger brother severely, simply removing him from all his land possessions in England rather than imprisoning him for treachery.

Knight with sword and triangular shield. (*Photo and copyright by Sirotci*)

Knight with *chapel de fer* helmet and padded gambeson. (*Photo and copyright by Sirotci*)

After having restored order in his kingdom, the Lionheart crossed to France in order to fight the forces of Philip Augustus. The King of France had attacked Normandy during Richard's captivity and had occupied the region of Vexin. Richard spent the following years building new castles in Normandy and skirmishing with the French. At the same time, he organized a grand alliance against his rival Philip that comprised Baldwin IX, Count of Flanders, and Sancho VI, King of Navarre. On the battlefield, the Angevin forces obtained several victories over the French. Philip was initially defeated at the Battle of Fréteval in 1194 and later at the larger Battle of Gisors in 1198. The latter saw the clash between 200 English knights and 300 mounted French fighters being decided by an audacious charge led by the Lionheart. In March 1199, Richard moved to Limousin in order to suppress a revolt by the local ruler, Aimar V of Limoges. The Lionheart was struggling to keep the Angevin Empire that he inherited from his father united, and understood that Philip's main target was the Duchy of Normandy. Consequently, he employed all his resources and personal energies to secure his position in northern France. On 26 March, while besieging a castle in Limousin, Richard was hit in the shoulder by the dart of a crossbow. The wound, which initially seemed curable, rapidly turned gangrenous. On 6 April 1199, in the arms of his mother, Eleanor of Aquitaine, Richard the Lionheart died. Since the king had no legitimate heirs, he was succeeded as monarch of England by his brother, John. The French territories of the Angevins rejected John's rule, an act that marked the beginning of the end for the empire created by Henry II.

Chapter 4

King John and the First Barons' War

Upon Richard's death there were two potential claimants to the English throne: John and the young Arthur I of Brittany, the son of John's elder brother, Geoffrey. John, however, was supported by most of the English aristocrats and backed by his mother, Eleanor of Aquitaine. As a result, he was crowned in Westminster soon after the death of his brother. Arthur was supported by the nobles of Brittany, Maine and Anjou, and had an ally in Philip Augustus, who was determined to continue his campaigns in Normandy against the new English monarch. Soon after becoming king, John had to defend the Duchy of Normandy from assaults by Arthur and Philip. He could count on the excellent castles that had been built by his brother, as well as the network of regional alliances that had been created by the Lionheart. Since neither side was able to gain the upper hand in the hostilities, John and Philip met to negotiate the terms for peace in January 1200, both being under strong pressure from the papacy. The resulting Treaty of Le Goulet was signed some months later, according to which Philip recognized John as the legitimate heir of Richard's French possessions and John recognized Philip as his feudal overlord in France. The new peace, however, was only short-lived, since in 1202 both sides resumed hostilities. At the beginning of the new war, King John adopted a defensive attitude similar to that of 1199: he avoided fighting a pitched battle against the French and limited himself to defending his strong castles. Normandy was also attacked again by two armies, the French one of Philip Augustus and a Breton force under Arthur. After some indecisive engagements, John decided to face Arthur on the open field and defeated him at the Battle of Mirebeau on 31 July 1202. This was the first important victory for the King of England, who was able to capture Arthur and most of his supporters. The young Duke of Brittany was killed some months later in order to eliminate a dangerous potential rival for John. At this point of the war, however, John started to experience serious difficulties. Since his armies were mostly made up of mercenaries recruited from Flanders and Brabant, his financial resources were becoming increasingly stretched. Meanwhile, he was not able to secure control over the territories of those that had supported Arthur.

An increasing number of Angevin nobles, who had been loyal to Richard the Lionheart, then started to abandon John. With Arthur's death and with the new king experiencing serious military difficulties, they began to see Philip Augustus as their new overlord. By this time the King of France was besieging Chateau Gaillard, the strongest fortification built by Richard the Lionheart to defend the borders of Normandy. John attempted to relieve the besieged garrison in the latter part of 1203, but his counter-offensive failed. The frustrated English monarch then moved to Brittany, where the population had started revolting against him. John crushed the Breton uprising with great determination, but could do little to improve his general military situation. King Philip, who could count on large feudal military forces, was gradually gaining the upper hand. In March 1204, after a long and complex siege, Chateau Gaillard was taken by the French. Some weeks after this event, Eleanor of Aquitaine died. John's forces in Normandy tried to establish a new defensive line after the fall of their main stronghold, but Philip was able to move around these defences and launch a devastating offensive against the very heart of Normandy without meeting significant resistance. By August 1204, the King of France had conquered the whole of Normandy and then continued his advance. He also invested Anjou and Poitou, which were occupied quite easily by the French thanks to the collaboration of the local nobles. By the end of the year, of the Angevin Empire's French territories only the Duchy of Aquitaine remained in John's hands. The military disasters of 1203 and 1204 greatly weakened the international position of the King of England, who had to secure the sea route connecting Aquitaine to England following the loss of the land one that crossed Normandy. In addition, John had to secure England against a potential French invasion. He reorganized his feudal forces in order to have a number of permanent troops at his disposal and built many new warships so that he could control the English Channel. His main objective, however, was reconquering Normandy.

By 1212, King John could already count on a large fleet of over 100 vessels, made up of three main components: royal galleys built during recent years, smaller warships provided by the coastal centres of the Cinque Ports, and merchant ships converted to military use. John's new fleet was commanded by William of Wrotham and had Portsmouth as its main operational base. The new naval resources assembled by John, however, were mostly used for defensive purposes. Instead of attempting a landing in Normandy, William of Wrotham was tasked with protecting the southern coast of England from any attack by the French. King John wanted to reconquer Normandy by attacking it from the south. His plan was to raise substantial land forces in Aquitaine and to use these to attack the French in Poitou (a key region located north of Aquitaine and south of Normandy). In 1206, John went to Poitou to organize an initial offensive against Poitou, but was diverted by a minor campaign on the southern border of Aquitaine against Alfonso VIII of Castile. After losing

Knight with *chapel de fer* helmet and padded gambeson. (*Photo and copyright by Sirotci*)

precious time, the English monarch finally attacked in Poitou and took the important city of Angers. When Philip Augustus moved south to intercept John, the campaign ended in stalemate and a truce of two years was stipulated between the two kings. This brief period of peace was employed by John to gather more financial resources for a new attack on Normandy. He also concluded important military alliances with Otto IV (a pretender to the crown of the Holy Roman Empire) and several major French aristocrats (Renaud of Boulogne and Ferdinand of Flanders among others). In 1213, Philip Augustus took the initiative before John and sent his elder son, Louis, to invade Flanders. Philip's plan was to take control of the strategically vital Flemish ports in order to organize an invasion of England. John was thus forced to use his new fleet for the first time, launching a pre-emptive strike against the French naval forces that were anchored in the harbour of Damme. The English raid was a success and resulted in the destruction of most of Philip's vessels. Consequently, the French plans for an invasion of England had to be abandoned.

France was not the only external enemy of King John, who also had to fight in Scotland and Wales during

Knight with great helm. (*Photo and copyright by Sirotci*)

his reign. In 1209, the monarch was informed of William I of Scotland's intention of forming an alliance with the French. As a result, he decided to invade Scotland and after a very rapid campaign he forced the Scottish king to sign the Treaty of Norham. According to its terms, William I abandoned all his expansionist ambitions against northern England and accepted the payment of a large sum of money to King John. In Wales, John had to face a major uprising in 1211, caused by a succession crisis that took place in one of the Welsh princedoms. In order to restore order and to reconfirm English political influence, John mounted a large-scale invasion. It was a great success. For the first time, a royal English army marched across Wales and reached the very heartland of the Welsh princedoms. Soon after the end of the expedition, however, the local warlords regained most of their previous autonomy and the situation in Wales reverted to the *status quo*. Meanwhile, John remained Lord of Ireland for the entire duration of his reign. His Irish policy was very simple: he tried to expand English territorial possessions in every possible way, whether through diplomacy or minor military interventions. In 1210, John landed in Ireland at the head of a sizeable army in order to crush a rebellion of the local English barons, who had revolted against his rule. The expedition was a success and order was restored, but John was not able to extend his authority over that part of Ireland which was still independent from England. John had been unable to change the relationships existing between his kingdom and the Celtic nations: the border issues with Scotland remained, despite a temporary success, Wales continued to be a rebellious country enjoying a high degree of political autonomy, and the English position in Ireland remained quite precarious.

King John's reign was also characterized by a difficult relationship with the papacy. Since 1205, in fact, the monarch had become involved in a dispute with Pope Innocent III over the choice of the new Archbishop of Canterbury that almost caused the English king's excommunication. The diplomatic crisis with the papacy ended only in 1213, when an agreement was finally reached. For several years, however, Innocent III was one of John's main enemies, plotting against him together with King Philip Augustus.

In 1214, King John organized his last military campaign in continental Europe, again with the objective of taking Normandy back from Philip of France. This time he appeared to have a good chance of victory, since he had been able to organize a very strong anti-French military alliance. Otto IV had finally been proclaimed Holy Roman Emperor by a good portion of the German princes, and thus was now ready to help his English ally with substantial military resources. Renaud of Boulogne and Ferdinand of Flanders, both being extremely worried by their king's projects for political centralization, were also determined to fight on the side of King John.

Knight with hunting dog. (*Photo and copyright by Sirotci*)

Knight with padded gambeson. (*Photo and copyright by Sirotci*)

The English monarch came up with a very complex military plan: he, at the head of an army mostly made up of mercenaries, would attack from Aquitaine by crossing Poitou and would menace the city of Paris, while his three allies (Otto, Renaud and Ferdinand) would assemble an army in Flanders and attack the French from the north-east. The allied forces in Flanders would be supported by an English contingent commanded by William Longespée, one of John's most loyal and experienced military commanders. Initially everything worked well for King John. Setting out from Aquitaine, he outmanoeuvred the French forces facing him that were commanded by Prince Louis of France, and the English were able to reconquer the County of Anjou by the end of June.

Meanwhile, in the north, Philip Augustus had to mobilize his troops very rapidly in order to face the menace presented by Otto's large army. The opposing forces met on 27 July on the plain of Bouvines, where one of the largest and most important battles of the Middle Ages was fought. Philip Augustus' army consisted of around 1,300 heavy knights (of whom 765 came from the lands of the royal domain) and 300 'mounted sergeants', supported by 3,160 infantrymen provided by the municipalities of northern France. The King of France could also count on 2,000 mercenary infantry, and thus his army numbered some 6,700 men. These were deployed on the field of battle into three divisions, known as 'battles' according to medieval military terminology. The right battle consisted of knights from Champagne, Burgundy and Picardy, as well as 150 mounted sergeants from Soissons. The central battle comprised knights from the lands of the royal domain as well as foot militiamen sent by the towns of northern France. The left battle consisted of Breton knights and other foot militia provided by the municipalities. Behind the French army was the bridge of Bouvines, the only means of retreat across an area of marshland, that was guarded by 150 mounted sergeants. The Imperial army of Otto comprised around 1,500 knights (including 650 from Flanders and 500 from Hainaut) plus 7,500 infantry (including several hundred English archers). Like King Philip, the Holy Roman Emperor divided his troops into three divisions, or battles. The left battle consisted of Flemish knights, supported by foot soldiers from Flanders and Hainaut. The central battle was made up of Saxon knights as well as infantrymen from Germany and Brabant who were equipped with long pikes. The right battle comprised English knights and foot soldiers from Brabant, and was commanded by William Longespée, Earl of Salisbury. The English archers were deployed as a reserve on the extreme right flank of the Imperial army. The Battle of Bouvines began with an attack by the French right flank, launched by the 150 lightly armoured mounted sergeants against the Flemish knights opposing them. This assault was easily repulsed by Otto's men, but was followed by a second attack led by the knights of Champagne. This was also

Knight with great helm decorated
for a tournament. (*Photo and
copyright by Sirotci*)

Heavy infantryman with spear and round shield. (*Photo and copyright by Sjórvaldar Vikings*)

halted by the Flemish knights, who then took the initiative. To stop the Flemish advance, the French had no choice but to launch several frontal charges with all their knights of the left division, until the enemy ranks were broken after three hours of bitter fighting. In the centre, the French urban militia were easily crushed by Otto's elite German knights. King Philip, who was in the centre of his line, was unhorsed during this phase of the battle, and was saved only with great difficulties by his knights. The French also launched several frontal charges in this sector with all their available knights until Otto's men were finally pushed back. The emperor ran the risk of being captured and his personal banner was taken by the French knights. On the Imperial left, William Longespée, after some initial success, was unhorsed and captured: his soldiers, demoralized, fled from the battlefield after having seen very little action. When the allied forces started to abandon the battlefield, only a force of 700 pikemen from Brabant resisted against the advancing French by forming a defensive ring. The Imperial infantry, led by Reginald of Boulogne, repulsed all the attacks of the French cavalry and gained some precious time for the retreat of their comrades until being completely crushed. The Battle of Bouvines had been a hard-fought victory for Philip Augustus. The enemy army that had invaded northern France was completely destroyed and King John's plans were frustrated. Having no hope of continuing his campaign from Aquitaine, John made peace with the King of France: Anjou was returned to Philip, and John even paid economic compensation to his rival. The Battle of Bouvines also had important consequences for the political situation in England, since it destroyed all hopes for a restoration of the Angevin Empire. King John's position had become extremely precarious in his home realm, with the English barons ready to take advantage of the situation in order to pursue their own interests.

Like his predecessors Henry II and Richard, John justified his political actions as king on the basis that he was above the law since he possessed the quality of 'divine majesty'. This concept was widespread in Europe during the first half of the Middle Ages, but was not as widely accepted as one might expect. Many intellectuals of the time did not consider the nature of kingship as being divine; they believed, instead, that monarchs should rule in accordance with custom and the law. In England, this vision of royal power was well established by the beginning of the thirteenth century and was sustained by many of the most powerful barons. According to their point of view, the king had to take council with the nobles before making any major decision. The personal power of the king was exerted through a sophisticated system of administration, which comprised a series of different offices: the Chancery kept written records of all official communications sent and received by the king, the Treasury dealt with financial income and the Exchequer handled all

Heavy infantryman with sword and dagger. (*Photo and copyright by Confraternita del Leone/Historia Viva*)

Heavy infantryman with mask helmet and falchion sword. (*Photo and copyright by Pisa Ghibellina*)

financial expenditure. In addition, there were the judges who administered justice across the kingdom according to their different jurisdictions. Royal courts sometimes played a significant role in local law cases, especially after King John increased the professionalism of his local officials such as the sergeants and the bailiffs. Before the ascendancy of King John, especially under Richard the Lionheart, local justice had been mostly administered by the feudal lords; as a result, the king's administrative reforms were very unpopular among the aristocrats, who had no intention of renouncing part of their personal power. Like Henry II and Richard, John organized a peripatetic court that travelled around the realm for most of the year in order to have direct control of the territory and of the various barons.

During his reign, King John spent enormous sums of money to fund his military expeditions in France. Since the English nobles were not willing to fight by his side in Normandy or Aquitaine, he had to rely – quite massively – on the use of foreign mercenaries, which only augmented the cost of the war effort. Due to the ongoing hostilities with France, John also built up a large military fleet in a very short period, and this too had a great impact on the finances of the realm. Like his predecessors, the king could count on three main sources of income to fund his military expeditions: revenues from the lands of the royal domain, or 'demesne'; taxation raised through royal rights from the baronial lands; and money coming from direct taxation. During the first period of his reign, Richard the Lionheart had sold many properties of the royal domain in order to fund the Third Crusade, and thus the general value of the 'demesne' had become less significant. Since increasing the revenues from direct taxation was extremely difficult, John had no choice but to introduce new forms of indirect taxation based on feudal rights. The monarch, for example, created the so-called 'scutage system', according to which the nobles could avoid military service by sending a cash payment to the king. John also sold some royal feudal rights to his most loyal barons in order to earn more money. Generally speaking, the royal management of taxation was quite arbitrary, since it was heavily influenced by the king's personal attitude towards individual nobles. Debts owed to the crown by aristocrats who supported the monarch could be easily 'forgiven', while those owed by barons who opposed the policy of John were enforced with great regularity. Indirect taxation was particularly heavy under King John's reign, and this caused great malcontent among his barons: he levied scutage payments eleven times during his seventeen years of rule, which was unprecedented in English history. The monarch also maximized his right to demand relief payments when properties of the nobles (including castles) were inherited by their heirs. This was a further cause of malcontent, together with the sale of sheriff appointments. The new sheriffs spent large sums of money to purchase their appointments as royal officials, and usually made back their investment by increasing fines and penalties on the inhabitants of their territory. The king also sold charters for the creation of new towns and new markets across his realm, on a scale never seen before. He even introduced a new tax on income and movable goods during 1207. The lands of the barons who could not pay or refused to pay the new taxes of King John were usually confiscated. As a result of all these actions, John's economic and financial policy became particularly hated across the realm (especially after it became apparent that the king had no more chance of reconquering Normandy).

During the long struggle between John and the papacy, the crown confiscated all the properties and goods of the English clergymen who remained loyal to the Pope. By selling the seized monasteries and obtaining control over the treasures of the churches, King John was able to cover most of his military expenses. The controversy with the Pope came to an end only when the monarch agreed to recognize the candidate supported by the papacy as the new legitimate Archbishop of Canterbury. In exchange for this, however, John was to keep all the properties and goods that he had confiscated from the English clergy during recent years. The living conditions of the poorest subjects, most notably the peasants, were quite difficult at this time: a bad harvest, for example, could cause the death of an entire family. John did very little to improve the quality of life of the common people, paying attention only to the requests of London's inhabitants since they could influence the political life of the realm by revolting against the crown.

As was the case with his predecessors, John's power was based on his royal household. This included two separate groups of people who had different military and administrative functions. The first group was that of the *familiares regis*, who were the relatives or immediate friends of the monarch, followed him around the country and were part of the court. Generally speaking, the *familiares regis* all had important military functions and thus acted as 'field commanders' in case of war. The second group was the *curia regis*, which was made up of senior officials and agents who performed important administrative functions. As time passed, an increasing number of 'new men' (nobles of low rank) entered the exclusive circle of the *curia regis*; the *familiares regis* continued to be made up mostly of relatives or personal friends of the monarch. The English barons hated the members of the *curia regis* because they were more powerful than them but came from an inferior social class. In addition, many of these officials were experienced mercenaries from France and not subjects of the English crown. By reforming taxation and justice according to his own needs, King John created a new system of power that could easily destroy any baron who opposed his rule. John had a very negative opinion of most of his nobles, and thus preferred to follow the advice of his 'new men' instead of consulting the aristocrats before taking important decisions. When a baron was suspected of treason, he soon became the target of the king's *malevolentia*, or 'bad will': he could easily be exiled or even killed without any real juridical justification. As a result of all the political, administrative and economic reforms introduced by King John, the English barons started a major uprising against the crown in the hope of removing the hated monarch. Their plans began coming together soon after the Battle of Bouvines, which was a disaster for the international reputation of John. Seeing that the French territories of the Angevin Empire had been lost forever (with the exception of Aquitaine) and that they could count on the direct support of Philip Augustus, the barons initiated their revolt. Before the uprising latter could begin, King John held a council in London during January 1215 to discuss various potential reforms; meanwhile, he also began recruiting mercenaries from France.

After the talks came to nothing, the barons congregated at Northampton in May 1215 and officially renounced their feudal ties to King John. Robert Fitzwalter was chosen as their military leader. The troops assembled by the English nobles were collectively known as the 'Army of God', since the barons were sure they were fighting in the name of a superior moral authority. They marched on London and easily took the capital, as well as the important cities of Lincoln and Exeter. In this opening phase of the First Barons' War, the monarch tried to find a compromise with the mutinous nobles, since he was too weak militarily to confront them. He held a meeting with the rebel leaders in June 1215, not far from Windsor, during which the two sides agreed to create a charter that contained the political requests of the barons. This document, which later became known as the *Magna Carta*, or 'Great Charter', contained a wide proposal for political reform. It promised protection of church rights, protection from illegal imprisonment, access to swift justice, balanced taxation applied only with baronial consent and limitations on the indirect forms of feudal taxation (most notably on the scutage system). In practice, the Great Charter was a form of 'proto-constitution' created according to the mentality of the Middle Ages. A council of twenty-five barons was to be formed to monitor King John's adherence to the document, but the Army of God was to be disbanded and the city of London returned to the monarch's control. Since the king had no real intention of implementing the peace agreement that had been reached with the nobles, the barons did not demobilize their forces and did not surrender London. It had become clear that both sides were ready to fight. John appealed for help to Pope Innocent III, who excommunicated the rebel barons after declaring that the *Magna Carta* contained illegal and unjust requests.

King John, despite the numerical superiority of his enemies, was well prepared for war. He had recruited a substantial number of mercenaries and could count on

Heavy infantryman with
sword and rectangular
shield. (*Photo and copyright
by Confraternita del Leone/
Historia Viva*)

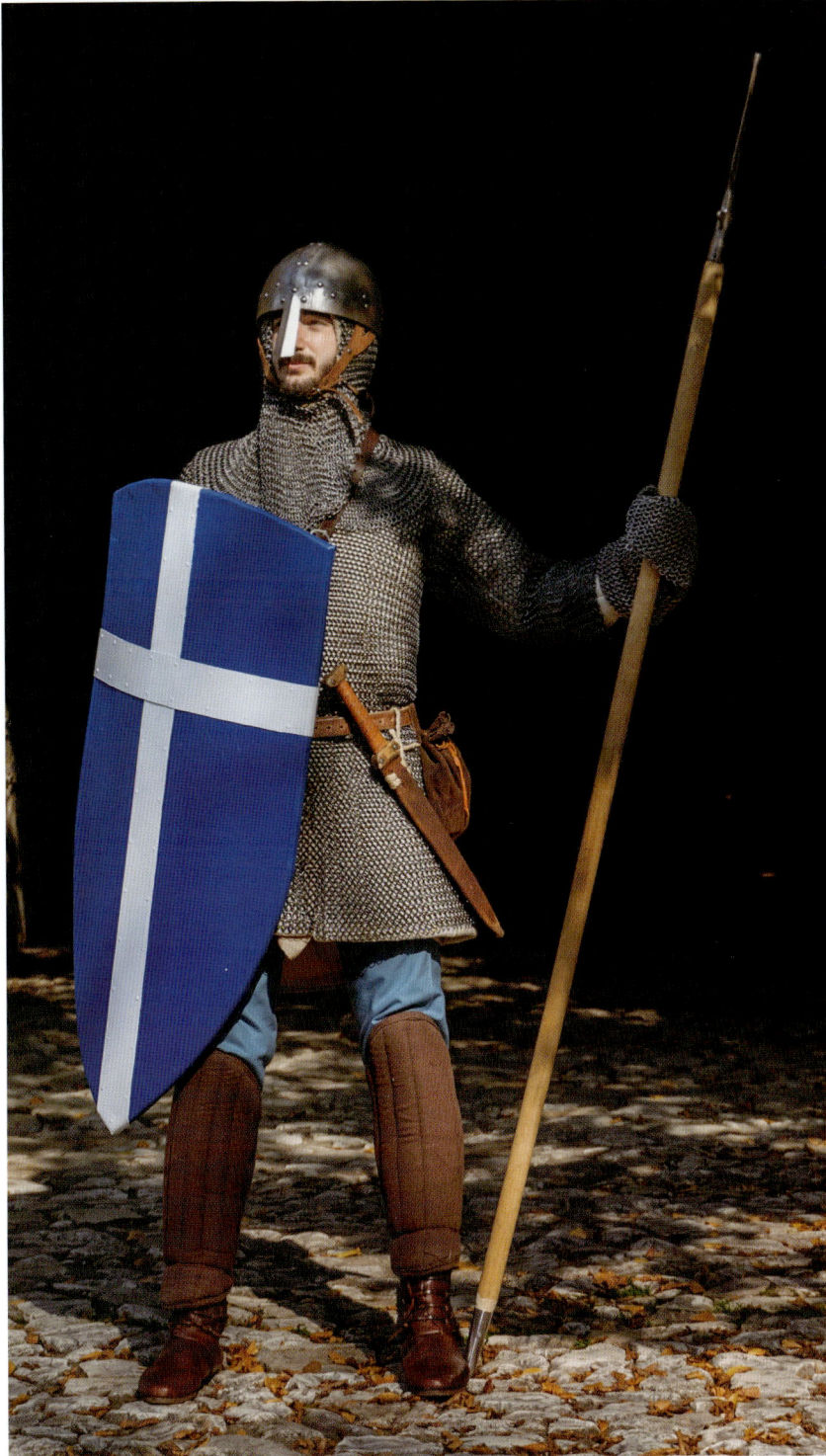

Heavy infantryman with spear and shield. (*Photo and copyright by Confraternita del Leone/Historia Viva*)

the support of the powerful Marcher Lords (nobles from the borders with Wales). In addition, the monarch controlled a network of strong royal castles and had large financial resources at his disposal. John's strategy was very simple: he intended to isolate and defeat the 'Army of God' in London before the King of France could land troops in southern England to support them. Philip Augustus and his young son, Louis, supported the English barons from the beginning of their rebellion. The revolt of the barons also exposed England to other external threats: a new rebellion broke out in the northern part of Wales, and Alexander II of Scotland crossed the border of northern England to support the rebels. King John reacted rapidly to these events, taking the castle of Rochester from his enemies in order to regain control over the south-eastern route to London. He then sent William Longespée (who had by now been freed) to retake the north-western route to the capital and himself moved north with most of his forces to ravage the lands of the local barons as well as to deal with Alexander II. John's campaign in the north was a triumph: he defeated the barons and recaptured most of northern England, pushing the Scottish troops back to Edinburgh. At this point, realizing that they were facing defeat, the rebellious English nobles invited Louis of France to support them. Philip Augustus' son intended to land in southern England in May 1216, so John sent his powerful fleet to intercept him. Unfortunately for the king, however, a series of storms dispersed his ships and the French were able to land unopposed in Kent. Louis took control of Kent quite easily, including the important royal castles of Canterbury and Rochester. On 25 July, the Anglo-French forces of the barons moved to the key castle of Dover, which was well-supplied and contained a large garrison. After a siege lasting three months, Louis was forced to abandon his attempt to take the castle in order to move on London. In addition to Dover, the castles of Windsor and Lincoln also resisted the besieging operations of the Anglo-French army. When a pitched battle between John and Louis seemed imminent, Alexander II invaded northern England again and thus the royal army had to move to intercept the Scottish forces (which had already occupied Carlisle). Being unable to crush the invading Alexander II and occupy London before the arrival of Louis, the king fell back to Winchester, where he started reorganizing his forces.

The French prince entered London after encountering very little resistance and was soon proclaimed (though not crowned) King of England. Alexander II of Scotland was also present at the ceremony and gave homage to Louis, since he held important fiefs in England. However, many barons slowly started to change their attitude towards their foreign ally. They had initially invited the French to help because they wanted to defeat John, but now England was running the risk of becoming a domain of Philip Augustus. Some of the leading nobles who had previously abandoned

Heavy infantryman with spear and kite shield. (*Photo and copyright by Confraternita del Leone/Historia Viva*)

King John, such as William Longespée, changed sides and rejoined the royalists. Despite the defection of numerous aristocrats who had initially supported him, Louis continued his conquest of England, advancing westwards and besieged the castle of Winchester which John had made his base. This was taken after ten days of fighting, but King John had already abandoned it. In September 1216, John launched

Heavy infantryman with
chainmail worn over padded
gambeson. (*Photo and copyright
by Confraternita del Leone/
Historia Viva*)

a strong counter-offensive, attacking eastwards between London and Cambridge in order to break up the positions of his enemies. While leading the offensive, however, the king contracted dysentery and fell ill. On 19 October 1216, the king died at the castle of Newark in Nottinghamshire. With his death, the main reason for the conflict ceased to exist. The barons, having achieved their objective without fighting a single pitched battle, then decided to expel Louis and the French from the country. Prince Henry, the son and heir of King John, was a child aged just 9 and thus was not perceived as a menace like the foreign prince. Most of the nobles abandoned their former French allies and crowned the young Henry in Gloucester Abbey. Louis still controlled London and a good portion of England, but his forces were now at a clear numerical disadvantage.

On 12 November 1216, the *Magna Carta* was officially reissued in the name of the new monarch, Henry III. The revised version of the original charter was sealed by the baron who had been made regent of the infant king, William Marshal. Although Marshal slowly managed to get most barons to abandon Louis, the civil war between the royalists and the French pretender to the throne of England lasted for another year. During the closing weeks of 1216, Louis occupied several important castles, but in early 1217 he decided to return to his father's kingdom in search of fresh reinforcements. To reach France he had to cross Sussex and Kent, where a strong resistance movement had gradually developed: he was attacked on several occasions during his journey and was ambushed at Lewes. Louis lost many of his men during these minor clashes, but before he could leave England a new French fleet arrived with reinforcements and supplies. Now that the barons were his enemies, Louis was becoming increasingly dependent on the men and supplies sent from France by his father, so he desperately needed to capture the port of Dover to use as his main naval base. The French prince besieged Dover for a second time, but once again he was unable to take it. While the French were concentrating their efforts against Dover, William Marshal attacked the forces of those barons who were still fighting on Louis' side near the castle of Lincoln in May 1217. In what became known as the Second Battle of Lincoln, 1,000 men assembled by Marshal were able to defeat 1,600 pro-Louis soldiers who were besieging the castle (whose garrison was loyal to Henry III). After the Second Battle of Lincoln, Louis decided to raise his second siege of Dover and went back to London with the reinforcements that he had received. Negotiations between Louis and William Marshal came to nothing and the hostilities continued. Several weeks later there was a decisive turn of the tide when a new French fleet that had been sent to support Louis was defeated by English warships at the Battle of Sandwich on 24 August 1217. The French fleet was commanded by Eustace the Monk, an adventurer who once belonged to a monastic order before becoming a

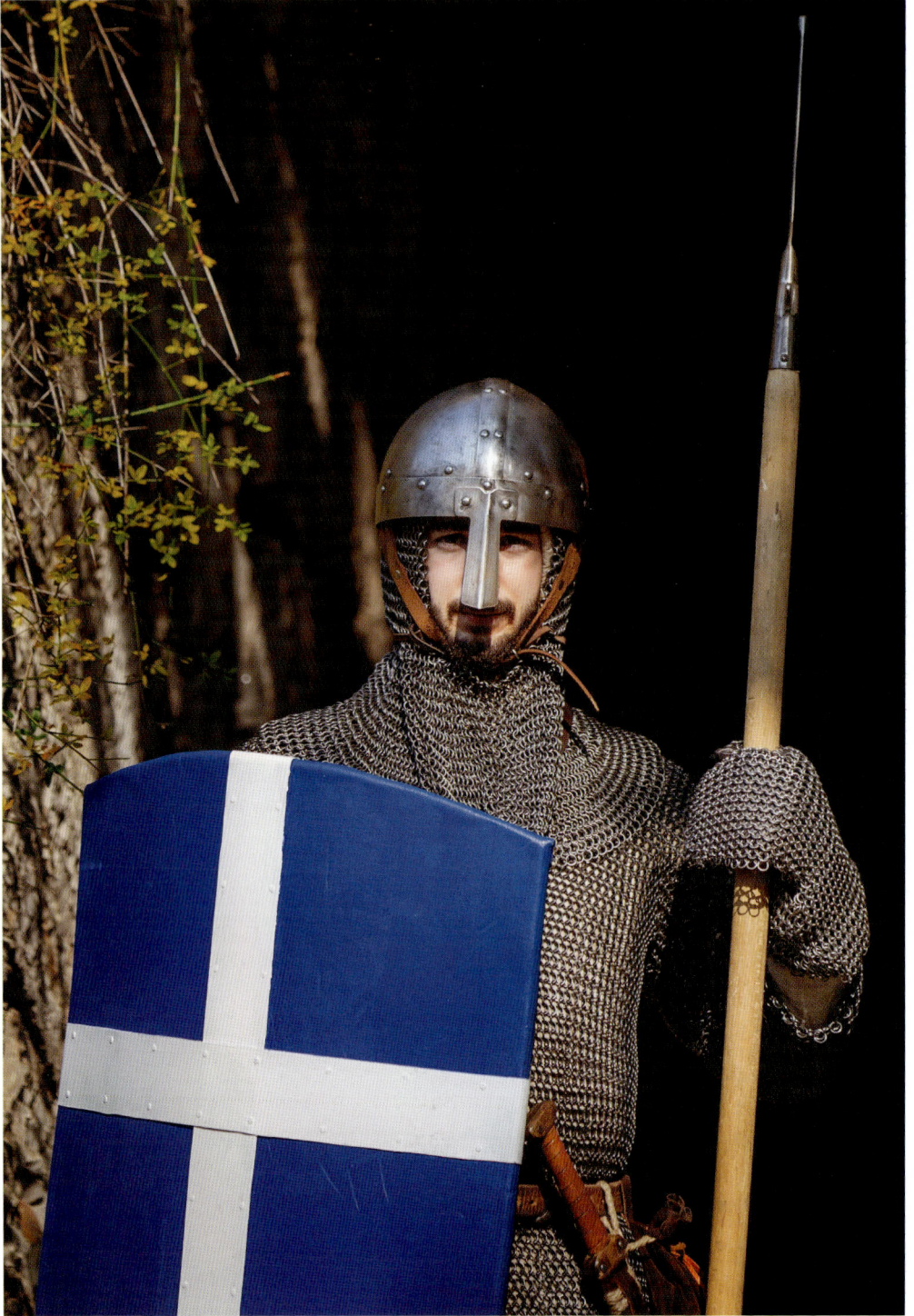

Heavy infantryman with helmet with nasal. (*Photo and copyright by Confraternita del Leone/Historia Viva*)

Heavy infantryman with mace and rectangular shield. (*Photo and copyright by Confraternita del Leone/ Historia Viva*)

pirate. During the years 1205–1208, Eustace and his companions had worked for King John, who gave the pirate leader the Channel Islands and permitted him to use Winchelsea as his main base in England. In 1212, however, the former monk changed sides and started to serve Philip Augustus. It was thanks to Eustace that Louis had been able to land in southern England to support the mutinous barons and that the French had captured the Cinque Ports.

In the late summer of 1217, Philip had sent a new fleet with reinforcements and supplies to England from Calais, commanded by Eustace the Monk. The crews of the English warships – which had been built by King John – now showed their valour. Commanded by Hubert the Burgh, they had just one order: to crush the French fleet. Initially, the sailors from the Cinque Ports, who had been treated very badly by King John, had no intention to fight against the French, but they were convinced to do so with the promise of great spoils should they destroy the French. Eustace the Monk, who was not formally the overall French commander, had eleven warships and seventy smaller transport vessels carrying supplies. The English fleet facing them had sixteen warships and twenty smaller auxiliary vessels. When the French armada sailed past Sandwich, the English fleet sailed out of the port and attacked them. Eustace was trying to reach the Thames estuary so that he could reinforce Louis in London. Soon after the start of the clash, the English warships gained the windward position and this gave them a great advantage. The English vessels were smaller than their French equivalents, but each of them had a contingent of archers, who killed many enemy sailors and soldiers from a distance before the French bowmen on Eustace's vessels could respond. After some very hard fighting, the French flagship was boarded by the English and Eustace was captured. He was later executed as a traitor. Defeated, the remaining French warships returned to Calais. Most of the transport vessels were captured by the English. The Battle of Sandwich, one of the greatest naval clashes of the Middle Ages, was decisive in determining the outcome of the First Barons' War. After the defeat, with the English in full control of the Channel, Philip Augustus stopped sending support for his son. Louis was totally cut off from France and abandoned by his remaining English supporters. On 12 September 1217, a peace treaty was signed at Kingston upon Thames, whereby Louis formally renounced all his claims to the throne of England in return for being allowed to return to France. Henry III, the new King of England, pardoned all the barons who had remained loyal to the French. England was again united and had avoided foreign occupation, and Henry III could now guide the realm with the decisive support of William Marshal.

Heavy infantryman with *chapel de fer* helmet and falchion sword. (*Photo and copyright by Antichi Popoli*)

Infantryman with padded
gambeson and kite shield.
(*Photo and copyright by
Confraternita del Leone/
Historia Viva*)

Chapter 5

The Long Reign of Henry III

With the end of the hostilities in 1217, William Marshal faced the task of rebuilding royal authority across large portions of England. The realm was in a state of complete disorder: the network of county sheriffs had collapsed, together with the juridical system, many unauthorized castles and fortifications had been built, the raising of taxes had become extremely difficult and many peasants were on the verge of starvation. The Kingdom of Scotland continued to menace northern England, while the Welsh Marches were threatened by the powerful Welsh leader Llywelyn of the Kingdom of Gwynedd, the most important of the Welsh princedoms. In 1211, after revolting against King John, Llywelyn had been defeated by the English, but during the following years he had been able to restore his power. In 1213, Llywelyn concluded an alliance with Philip Augustus and thereafter fought against England during the First Barons' War. By 1216 he had freed himself from any form of indirect English control and had transformed the Kingdom of Gwynedd into the dominant military power of Wales. In 1218, after his French allies had been expelled from England, Llywelyn signed a treaty with Henry III which confirmed him in possession of all his recent conquests, something that caused malcontent among the Marcher Lords (including William Marshal). In 1220, the son of William Marshal attacked Llywelyn with an army from Ireland, also receiving support from royalist forces. The conflict, which remained a local affair between the Marcher Lords and Llywelyn, ended in 1223 with the restoration of the *status quo*. In 1228, however, the Welsh warlord launched another attack against English lands, and this time the royal army had to intervene on a large scale in order to support the Marcher Lords. William Marshal had died in 1219 before completing the process of reforms that he had started as regent. Three men took over the running of the English government in place of Marshal: the Papal legate Pandulf Verraccio, Peter des Roches and Hubert de Burgh (who had commanded the English warships at the Battle of Sandwich). The ambitious Hubert removed Peter des Roches in 1221, accusing him of treason, and in the same year Pandulf of Verraccio was recalled to Rome, leaving Hubert as the only remaining regent. Like his predecessor, Hubert de Burgh experienced serious difficulties in dealing with Llywelyn in Wales, while also having to face several minor revolts of unruly barons.

The weakness of Henry III was apparent, since he still did not have complete control over his own kingdom, despite his regent's efforts. Hoping to take advantage of this situation, Louis of France, who had been crowned king after the death of his father, Philip Augustus, attacked the English territorial possessions in Aquitaine (which were by now reduced to the regions of Poitou and Gascony). Poitou was easily conquered by the French, the local nobles abandoning the young Henry III. Part of Gascony was also occupied, but in 1225 an English army was sent to France with orders to retake it. In exchange for providing their support to the capture of Gascony, the English barons obtained from Henry III the enacting of an enlarged and improved version of the *Magna Carta*. The young king assumed formal control of his government in January 1227 at the age of 19, richly rewarding Hubert de Burgh for his services and giving him many land possessions. Louis VIII had died in 1226, leaving the throne to his young son, Louis IX (who was just 12 years old), whose rule was not accepted by many French nobles, which caused the outbreak of several revolts in France. In 1228, some of the French aristocrats who were rebelling against Louis IX called upon Henry III to invade France. In particular, Peter I, Duke of Brittany, openly revolted against the young Louis and paid homage to the King of England. Following these events, Henry III took the decision to invade France in 1230. He set sail from Portsmouth at the head of a large force of English troops, who landed at Saint-Malo in Brittany, where they joined forces with their French allies. Henry attacked the County of Anjou, but made little progress. He then returned to Brittany before finally deciding to suspend his invasion of France after realizing that the support of the French nobles for his cause was insincere.

Following the failure of Henry III's invasion of France, Hubert de Burgh fell from power. Consequently, his old rival Peter des Roches returned to England and allied himself with the most powerful barons who were not happy with the king's rule. Henry, in order to avoid the outbreak of a major rebellion, had no choice but to order the arrest of Hubert (who was accused of robbery by his rivals) and to give the responsibilities of government to Peter. However, Peter used his new personal power only to punish his enemies, including William Marshal's son, Richard. A new civil war therefore broke out between Peter des Roches and Richard Marshal, which saw several barons supporting Marshal in defence of the rights contained in the Great Charter. Richard was the most important of the Marcher Lords and thus could count on significant military forces. In addition, he had vast land possessions in Ireland and even formed an alliance with the Welsh warlord Llywelyn. In 1234, the Archbishop of Canterbury intervened in order to stop the hostilities, which ended only when Peter de Roches was removed from his role and Richard Marshal died. The internecine conflict had negative consequences for Henry III's position in France, since Brittany

Infantryman with padded gambeson and spear. (*Photo and copyright by Confraternita del Leone/Historia Viva*)

Infantryman with padded gambeson and *chapel de fer* helmet. (*Photo and copyright by Confraternita del Leone/Historia Viva*)

was recaptured by the French while he was fighting in his own kingdom. After the events of 1230–1234, the English king decided to rule his realm in an autonomous way: the important post of Justiciar was left vacant inside the royal government, while the position of Chancellor was deprived of most of its original powers. All the most important decisions started to be taken directly by the king, who was influenced only by the advice of his closest friends. Despite such moves, Henry III was not a tyrannical monarch and respected the *Magna Carta* on most occasions during his long reign. He also held large gatherings of nobles at his royal court, which started to be commonly known as 'parliaments'. These usually took place periodically when the king wanted to raise some special taxes, one-off levies that were used to fund a particular royal project such as a military expedition. Over time, not only the barons participated in these parliaments but also some representatives of the middle class, who were sent to the court to pursue the interests of their home county. The network of royal sheriffs created by King John declined during Henry III's reign, with regional justice reverting to the control of the local nobles. This greatly affected the collection of taxes, since it became difficult for the monarch to exploit the large debts owed to the crown by the barons.

During 1242 and 1243, Henry III was involved in a new French conflict, known as the Saintonge War from the name of the region where it was fought. After having been lost by King John, the County of Poitou had been ruled by the French. Louis VIII had given it to his second oldest son, Alphonse, while as we have seen, his first son became his successor on the French throne as Louis IX. The Poitevin barons were unhappy with the idea of having the King of France's brother as their feudal overlord, and when Alphonse came of age, they revolted against him. The rebellion was led by the most powerful of the Poitevin nobles, Hugh X of Lusignan. The barons of Poitou wanted to have Richard of Cornwall, the younger brother of Henry III, as their count, and asked the English monarch to support them in their rebellion. Louis IX assembled a very large army to help his brother and marched against the castle of Montreuil-Bonnin that was the main stronghold of the Lusignan family. Meanwhile, Henry III raised a force of 30,000 soldiers and set sail from Portsmouth. The King of England wanted to retake Poitou, which he considered to be a first step towards the restoration of the empire that had been lost by his father. On 20 July 1242, a decisive battle was fought between the forces of Henry III and Louis IX at Taillebourg, near the River Charente. Both sides deployed some 20,000 infantry, but the French had 4,000 heavy knights and the English just 1,600. The English attacked first, but were soon repulsed, after which a counter-attack by the French knights proved devastating and decided the outcome of the clash, with the strategic bridge crossing the Charente being occupied by Louis' men. After their victory the French took the rebel city of

Infantryman with helmet with nasal and kite shield. (*Photo and copyright by Confraternita del Leone/ Historia Viva*)

Infantryman with spear and kite shield. (*Photo and copyright by Confraternita del Leone/Historia Viva*)

assemble a substantial army and marched on London, where the population revolted against the king and trapped him in the Tower of London. After he arrived in the capital, Simon assumed effective control of England, yet the general support that he had in these early weeks of the war soon disappeared when some barons – who opposed his personal supremacy – liberated Henry III. At this point the king tried to mediate with the rebels and appealed to Louis IX for arbitration. In January 1264, the King of France declared his support for Henry, but his offer of arbitration was not accepted by Simon de Montfort and the most radical barons. Fighting resumed in February, when the rebels attacked the royalist supporters in the Welsh Marches and defeated them. Hostilities continued with the siege of Northampton by the royalists. An attempt by the rebel barons to free the besieged city ended in failure. Simon went with most of his troops to Kent, where he started besieging the castle of Rochester, but the investment soon had to be abandoned when royalist forces started to advance on London. Unexpectedly, Henry III decided not to invest his capital but to move to Rochester in order to relieve the garrison. He then captured the towns of Tonbridge and Winchelsea from the rebels.

When Henry III moved into Sussex, he was confronted by Simon de Montfort and the two sides clashed at the Battle of Lewes on 14 May 1264. The king had a clear numerical advantage, commanding 10,000 men while the barons had just 5,000 knights and soldiers. The battle opened with an effective royalist charge led by Henry's son, Edward, which crushed one wing of the baronial army. The young prince, however, followed his defeated opponents in close pursuit and left his father alone on the battlefield. Henry was left with little choice but to order a general assault in the hope of breaking the enemy's strong defensive positions, which were located on higher ground. But the attack was repulsed by the reserves of Simon de Montfort, and the royalists were defeated, Henry fleeing the battlefield in an attempt to avoid further losses. After the reverse at Lewes, the king had to send Edward to Simon de Montfort as a hostage and was obliged to sign a document that recognized as a legitimate document the new Provisions of Oxford that had been written by the rebels. In May the following year, however, Edward escaped from baronial custody and was able to assemble a new royalist army. At this point of the war, several nobles abandoned Simon de Montfort and joined Edward, since they considered the reforms projected by their former leader potentially dangerous for the survival of the aristocracy. After these defections, Simon could not prevent the royalist conquest of Gloucester and thereafter decided to move into Wales in order to forge an alliance with the local warlords (who provided him with some military contingents). Edward proved to be an excellent military commander during this phase of the conflict, attacking the main stronghold of Simon, the castle of Kenilworth, and besieging it with great determination.

Infantryman with spear and padded gambeson. (*Photo and copyright by Confraternita del Leone/Historia Viva*)

Infantryman with axe and kite shield. (*Photo and copyright by Confraternita del Leone/Historia Viva*)

The rebel barons responded by crossing the River Severn in a bid to reach Kenilworth to lift the siege. The royalist army, however, moved to intercept Simon de Montfort, leading to the decisive Battle of Evesham being fought on 4 August 1265. The royalists again had a clear numerical advantage, with Edward fielding 10,000 men and Simon de Montfort just 5,000. The young prince had learned from past experience and thus occupied the higher ground on the battlefield before the arrival of his enemies. The barons attacked first and invested the centre of the royalist army, but after some initial success, their Welsh contingents abandoned the battle. Edward rapidly surrounded his numerically inferior enemy and a terrible cavalry clash began. This soon became a massacre, with many of the barons being killed. The usual practice of the time of capturing enemy nobles in order to obtain a ransom was temporarily abandoned at Evesham, and Simon de Montfort and one of his sons were killed on the battlefield. Victory was complete for Edward, who was now ready to rule his realm as a king in place of his old father (who played no significant role in this final part of the conflict). The war lasted for several more months, the rebels continuing to defend their strongholds with desperate determination. In order to avoid further bloodshed, Henry III drafted a proclamation known as the Dictum of Kenilworth, according to

Infantryman with *chapel de fer* helmet and padded gambeson. (*Photo and copyright by Confraternita del Leone/Historia Viva*)

Infantryman with sword and helmet with nasal. (*Photo and copyright by Confraternita del Leone/Historia Viva*)

which all rebels could obtain royal pardon and regain their confiscated lands upon payment of a fine. On 14 December, the defenders of the castle of Kenilworth surrendered and accepted the terms of the Dictum. The final groups of rebels continued to fight until the summer of 1267, when they gave up their arms at the Isle of Ely, their last stronghold. Some months after these events, in November, the Statute of Marlborough replaced the Provisions of Oxford with the previous and more moderate Provisions of Westminster. In that same autumn, Henry also made peace with the Welsh princes who had supported the rebel barons. The last years of Henry's long reign saw him increasingly infirm, with Edward starting to play a more prominent role in the government of the realm. The king died on 16 November 1272 at Westminster, while Edward was fighting against the Muslims in the Eighth Crusade. The new king came back to England several months later.

Chapter 6

The Wars of Edward I

After being crowned King of England on 19 August 1274, Edward I soon turned his attention to the frontiers of his realm as he had just one ambitious objective in mind: making England the dominant power of the British Isles by conquering the territories of Wales, Scotland and Ireland. The first targets of the new expansionist policy of England were the princedoms of Wales, which had been at war with the Crown on several occasions since the days of William the Conqueror. As we have seen, the Marcher Lords had gradually been able to conquer a good portion of southern Wales, while the northern region of the country was still dominated by various independent local kingdoms. The most important of these was Gwynedd, which was the leading military power of Wales after it transformed the smaller princedoms of Powys and Deheubarth into tributary states. The princes of Gwynedd assumed the honorific title of 'Prince of Wales' when ascending their throne, and their authority was also recognized by the English kings. By the time of Edward I's coronation, Gwynedd was ruled by Llywelyn ap Gruffudd, who was a strong and experienced military leader like his predecessor Llywelyn the Great. In 1267, the Welsh princes had signed a peace treaty with Henry III, but soon resumed hostilities against the Marcher Lords. The Marcher Lords were unhappy with the crown's policy for Wales, since they were convinced that the right moment had come to finally conquer the country. For decades, the English had fought wars of expansion on the continent in the hope of consolidating the Angevin territorial possessions in France, but now that the kings of France were too strong to be defeated, English expansionism had to find new objectives. Wales and Ireland were obvious choices, since they had already been partly occupied over recent centuries. In 1274, Edward just needed a *casus belli* to attack Gwynedd, and he rapidly found it: two Welsh nobles attempted to assassinate Llywelyn, but their plans failed and they then defected to the English. One of them was Llywelyn's younger brother. The Welsh prince thus refused to offer his formal homage to the King of England, since Edward was supporting his internal enemies. In November 1276, war was declared between the two states.

In July 1277, Edward I launched his first invasion of Wales at the head of an army comprising 15,000 men, 9,000 of these being Welshmen who were opposed to Llywelyn's rule or who came from rival minor princedoms. The campaign had no pitched battles, since the Welsh were not used to fighting on the open field against large, well-organized English armies comprising a good number of heavy knights. Cavalry was a very minor component of the Welsh armies, which were mostly made up of light infantry skirmishers and archers. In a pitched battle, the Welsh light infantry had no hope of defeating the English heavy cavalry, but the sturdy Welsh fighters were very effective in launching hit-and-run attacks and using guerrilla tactics. They had a perfect knowledge of their homeland, the nature of which was still very wild, and thus could stage deadly ambushes and incursions against the invaders. Nevertheless, Llywelyn could not count upon widespread popular support and thus had no choice but to surrender without having fought a single proper battle. According to the Treaty of Aberconwy that was signed in November 1277, Gwynedd could no longer exert any form of political influence over the other Welsh princedoms, but remained independent of England. War broke out again in 1282, but this time it was fought with greater intensity. Edward had only launched a punitive expedition in 1277; now he wanted to occupy Wales in a more permanent way. The Welsh understood this and thus united all their forces to resist the invasion. The first phase of the conflict was particularly favourable to the Welsh, who obtained a couple of minor victories and staged a series of effective ambushes against the English. On 11 December 1282, however, Llywelyn and his army of 7,000 warriors were decisively defeated at the Battle of Orewin Bridge, where the arrows of the English archers and a charge by the English heavy knights killed hundreds of Welsh fighters, including Llywelyn. The Welsh warlord had made a fatal mistake in deciding to face the English on the open field. Following this clash, which proved decisive for the history of the British Isles, Gwynedd was rapidly occupied by Edward I.

In 1284, with the Statute of Rhuddlan, the Principality of Wales was incorporated into the Kingdom of England, being given a new administrative system with counties policed by sheriffs. In order to secure his possession over the newly conquered territories, Edward I initiated a full-scale colonization of Wales by building a series of new towns and castles across the country. Many English migrants were encouraged to move to Wales in order to populate the new settlements. The network of castles created by the English was particularly strong, being designed to prevent any future uprising. The title of Prince of Wales was now given to the heir to the English throne, starting from Edward I's son, Edward (the future Edward II). From an administrative point of view, the territory of Wales was partitioned between the crown and the English barons who had supported the conquest of the country (most notably the Marcher Lords). Those local rulers of central Wales who had fought on Edward's side retained their territorial possessions, but they were no longer princes since they were transformed into fiefs of the English crown. Within a few years the Welsh lands

Infantryman with *chapel de fer* helmet and axe. (*Photo and copyright by Confraternita del Leone/Historia Viva*)

Infantryman with *chapel de fer* helmet and mace. (*Photo and copyright by Confraternita del Leone/Historia Viva*)

underwent a radical process of change, with feudalism introduced together with English common law, while Welsh law continued to be used only for some civil cases and thus gradually disappeared. There were several Welsh rebellions during Edward I's reign, most notably in 1287 and in 1294: these, however, were all crushed by the English mostly thanks to the presence of their strong, stone-built castles, which the Welsh insurgents were unable to capture. By conquering Wales, Edward had eliminated one of the main elements menacing the stability of his realm's borders, while also obtaining the unconditioned loyalty of the powerful Marcher Lords.

Edward was an excellent monarch from many points of view. Within a few years he restored order in his kingdom after the disastrous experiences of the Second Barons' War and re-established royal authority over the nobility. He fought against all the abuses of power committed by royal officials in the various regions, and clamped down on the abuses of the nobility with the same energy. The king also revised the rights enjoyed by the barons in order to understand if some of them were abusing their power. In addition, he started to involve various new social groups in the administration of the realm. During his reign the role played by merchants became increasingly important; in exchange for this, however, they had to pay customs duties to the crown, and thus their money was used by Edward to fund his military campaigns. In 1295, continuing his process of reforms, the king opened parliament meetings to knights and representatives of the boroughs, and as a result, the common people started to be involved in major political decisions.

After completing the conquest of Wales, Edward turned his attention to Scotland. Broadly speaking, Anglo-Scottish relations over the previous decades had been quite positive, with the Scottish monarchs having renounced their expansionist ambitions over northern England. Between 1281 and 1284, however, the three children of Alexander III of Scotland all died, then in 1286 Alexander also died and the Scottish crown was thus given to his granddaughter, Margaret, who was just three years old at the time. The international position of Scotland was severely damaged by these unexpected events, which Edward I took as an opportunity to exert his influence over the Scottish monarchy. In 1286, the Treaty of Birgham was signed between England and Scotland, whereby it was agreed that Margaret would marry the English king's son, Edward, but that the Kingdom of Scotland would remain free from English overlordship. In the autumn of 1290, however, before she could even be crowned, Margaret fell ill and died, leaving the country without an obvious heir. A very complex succession crisis thus began, which is commonly known as the 'Great Cause'. As many as fourteen different potential heirs put forward their claims to the title of King of Scotland, but it soon became apparent that the dynastic battle for the destiny of Scotland would be fought between just two pretenders: John Balliol and

Infantryman with
padded gambeson
and spear. (*Photo
and copyright by
Confraternita del
Leone/Historia
Viva*)

Infantryman with camail and rectangular shield. (*Photo and copyright by Confraternita del Leone/ Historia Viva*)

Robert Bruce. Since the realm was on the verge of civil war, the Scottish aristocrats asked Edward I to conduct the proceedings of the succession process, although they did not ask him to arbitrate the long-running dispute in a direct way.

The final decision would be made by 104 auditors: forty appointed by Balliol, forty by Bruce and twenty-four selected by Edward I from senior members of the Scottish nobility. Edward, determined to become the overlord of Scotland, decided to help the Scottish aristocrats only to pursue his own political interests. He insisted that, if he was to settle the dynastic contest, he had to be recognized as the Kingdom of Scotland's feudal overlord. The Scottish nobles were initially reluctant to make such an important concession to the English king, but they eventually agreed that the realm should be handed over to Edward until a rightful heir could be found. After lengthy discussions, under the heavy influence of the English monarch, the auditors made their decision in favour of John Balliol on 17 November 1292. Once the new Scottish king was chosen, however, Edward refused to give up his control over Scotland, and Balliol soon became a 'puppet' in his hands while Scottish administration started to be managed by the English crown. This situation was unacceptable to the Scottish nobles, who were even required to provide troops to Edward for his military campaigns. Consequently, a major rebellion broke out in Scotland, with Carlisle being attacked. Edward responded by launching a massive invasion of the country in 1296. After sacking Berwick-upon-Tweed, he besieged the important castle of Dunbar. The Scots sent a relief force to the besieged stronghold, but this was routed by the English heavy cavalry at the Battle of Dunbar. While this was not a large clash – consisting only of a fight between two small groups of heavy knights – it caused the surrender of the Dunbar garrison. In addition, it showed the great tactical superiority that the English heavy cavalry had over their Scottish adversaries. After these defeats, Edward I advanced unopposed into the heart of Scotland and deposed Balliol, who was then imprisoned in the Tower of London. English officials took over the reins of government in Scotland, while Edward returned to England. The final destiny of Scotland, however, had not yet been decided.

The military campaigns of Edward I put great financial demands on his subjects, especially with the introduction of an unpopular additional duty on wool that damaged the livelihoods of many merchants. The fiscal demands of the crown also caused resentment among the nobles and the clergy. In 1294, the king demanded a grant of one half of all clerical revenues in order to fund his military expeditions; this was agreed, despite some opposition, and was followed by a second demand a few months later. In 1296, however, the attitude of the English clergy changed radically when the *Clericis laicos* papal bull was promulgated, which prohibited the clergy from paying taxes to any authority without receiving explicit consent from the

Pope. Fearing negative consequences for himself, the Archbishop of Canterbury did nothing to apply the papal bull in England, and thus the resistance of the clergy to Edward's taxation did not last long. Despite the opposition from the clergymen and nobles, Edward I was finally able to fund a continental expedition in 1297. Three years before this, the Count of Flanders, Guy, had tried to conclude an alliance with Edward by arranging a marriage between his daughter, Philippa, and the Prince of Wales. This move, however, had been perceived as a menace to the stability of his realm by the new King of France, Philip IV, who imprisoned Guy and forced him to call off the planned marriage. The County of Flanders had a very special political status at the time: its rulers paid homage to both the King of France and the Holy Roman Emperor, while English merchants also had some very strong commercial interests in Flanders. In 1296, the most important cities of the region were taken under French protection, at which point Guy asked for Edward I's help. However, a large French army invaded the County of Flanders in 1297 with orders to annex it to Philip IV's domains. Initially, the English tried to support their Flemish allies by attacking the French from Aquitaine, but they were unsuccessful. Therefore, in August 1297, Edward I landed with 900 knights and 7,500 infantry on the Flemish coast. After several weeks of fighting that saw no major engagements, the mediation of the Pope led to the signing of an armistice in October. Edward left the continent without having achieved any significant result, which was largely due to the fact that a major uprising had just begun in Scotland and the king had to deal with it.

During the previous months, discontent had been growing in Scotland, with the new English administrators being particularly hated by the local population. Two new Scottish leaders then emerged who were to play an important role in the revolt: Andrew de Moray and William Wallace. The first was the son of an important noble and had been captured by the English during the Battle of Dunbar. After managing to escape, he gathered a group of insurgents who started to attack the English using hit-and-run tactics. The activities of the insurgents were particularly successful and freed the entire province of Moray from Edward I's men. William Wallace, meanwhile, was a minor noble who rose to prominence in May 1297 when he killed the English sheriff of Lanark and started his own rebellion against the foreigners. When news of the revolt initiated by William rippled throughout Scotland, thousands of free men – notably Highlanders – rallied to him and greatly enlarged the forces at his command. Wallace soon gained the support of the Bishop of Glasgow and Sir William Douglas, a respected noble: what had begun as a popular but local revolt was transformed into a national rebellion. William obtained a series of victories and occupied Scone, the seat of the English-appointed Justiciar of Scotland, whereupon Edward I decided to intervene in order to restore his control over the northern part of

Infantryman with padded gambeson and spear. (*Photo and copyright by Confraternita del Leone/ Historia Viva*)

Scotland. The king ordered Robert Bruce to attack William Douglas' possessions in Lanarkshire, but while on the march the pretender to the Scottish throne decided to disobey the English king and join the rebellion. The revolt was becoming a full-scale war, with Robert Bruce's example being followed by most of the Scottish nobles. Meanwhile, Moray and Wallace continued to raise and train an increasing number of free men. They attacked the English on numerous occasions, and in a relatively short time forced the invaders south of the River Forth, leaving Edward's forces in possession of only the castle of Dundee. William Wallace then initiated a siege of the castle, but was soon informed that an English army under the Earl of Surrey was marching against him. At this point the Scottish leader, who had united his forces with those of Moray, decided to face the English on the open field in order to defend the bridge that crossed the Forth at Stirling.

On 11 September 1297, the iconic Battle of Stirling Bridge was fought. From a military point of view, Wallace's decision to fight a pitched clash against the English was extremely audacious: his forces consisted of just 6,000 infantry and 300 knights, while the Earl of Surrey had 7,000 footmen and 2,000 heavy cavalry. Until that moment, at least in the British Isles, an infantry force had never been able to defeat a strong contingent of feudal knights on the open field. Foot soldiers were not trained to fight in close formation, and thus had no chance of

Infantryman with *chapel de fer* helmet and camail.
(*Photo and copyright by Antichi Popoli*)

stopping a cavalry charge conducted by knights equipped with chainmail. The Scottish forces, however, had a great tactical advantage at Stirling, as the English knights had to cross the narrow bridge in order to attack their defensive positions. Wallace and Moray allowed the English to cross the bridge unmolested during the first phase of the battle, but when the number of English soldiers who had crossed the river reached 2,000, the Scottish troops launched a furious attack. The English knights who had completed the crossing charged against the Scottish infantry, but they were too few and were repulsed. At this point, the Scottish soldiers gained control of the eastern side of the bridge and encircled those English soldiers who had crossed the river. What followed was a massacre, with all 2,000 English knights and infantry who were trapped being killed. Although the bulk of the Earl of Surrey's army remained intact, and the English commander could have launched a fresh attack, his initial confidence had evaporated. He thus ordered the bridge to be destroyed and retreated towards Berwick. The Lowlands of Scotland had been abandoned to the rebels, who had obtained a first major victory over the English. The Battle of Stirling Bridge was particularly important from a psychological point of view, since it showed that the English

Archer with longbow. (*Photo and copyright by Confraternita del Leone/Historia Viva*)

Archer with corselet and axe. (*Photo and copyright by Confraternita del Leone/Historia Viva*)

heavy knights could be defeated by the Scottish infantry. During the clash, however, Andrew Moray was severely wounded and died a few days later. During the following weeks, William Wallace expelled the last English contingents from Scotland and organized an invasion of northern England. He entered Northumberland and pillaged the region without meeting any opposition.

In March 1298, after returning to Scotland, William was appointed 'Guardian of the Kingdom' in the name of the exiled King John Balliol. Meanwhile, Edward I was reorganizing his forces for a new attack against Scotland and had established his main base at York. The English invasion began in July and culminated with the Battle of Falkirk. The English army assembled by Edward comprised 2,000 heavy cavalry, 10,000 Welsh footmen, 2,000 archers and 500 mercenary crossbowmen. William Wallace commanded 4,000 infantry, who were supported by 1,000 cavalry and 1,000 archers. The 4,000 Scottish foot soldiers were all equipped as spearmen and were organized into four 'hedgehogs' known as 'schiltrons', compact close formations, very similar to the infantry phalanxes of Antiquity. Since their members were armed with long pikes, they were specifically designed to resist cavalry charges. During recent months, Wallace had greatly improved the training of his infantrymen, transforming them into an elite combat force. The English knights had never faced an infantry contingent of the same quality as the schiltrons, and thus had no idea of their tactics. Wallace filled the gaps between his four infantry formations with archers, and deployed his small cavalry force behind the schiltrons as a reserve. He occupied a strong defensive position and had no intention of abandoning it. Edward ordered a general charge of his cavalry, which was organized into four 'battles' or brigades and advanced in echelon formation. For the first time in the military history of the British Isles, a massive charge of feudal cavalry was blocked and defeated by infantry, the spearmen of the schiltrons repulsing the enemy assaults with their forest of pikes and killed a great number of English knights. After the defeat of his best troops, Edward did not abandon the battlefield but instead decided to attack the schiltrons with his excellent longbowmen, who fired thousands of arrows against the static infantry formations of the Scots, who provided a very easy target for them. Edward's mercenary crossbowmen also attacked the enemy infantry with their deadly darts. The Scottish footmen suffered extremely severe losses during this phase of the battle and their formations lost cohesion, and when the Welsh infantry and English cavalry launched a second attack, the schiltrons were broken up and the surviving Scottish infantry had to abandon the field. Edward had won the Battle of Falkirk thanks to his archers, but his cavalry had suffered serious losses and been humiliated by a contingent of 'plebeian' infantry. Despite eventually emerging victorious, Edward decided to leave Scotland after the battle and returned to York.

In May 1300, the King of England set in motion a new campaign against Scotland, but this only resulted in minor skirmishing and ended with a truce that was sponsored by the Pope. Meanwhile, the Scottish nobles had started to fight among themselves in order to determine the identity of their next king. Hoping to gain advantage from this situation, the English organized a new invasion of Scotland in 1301 and assembled two armies. Once again, however, Edward made very little progress against the Scots, and was forced to halt his campaign after accepting another truce. In November 1302, hostilities resumed once more, with some minor victories for the Scots. Meanwhile, Robert Bruce had decided – temporarily – to support Edward I in the hope of being chosen by the English monarch as the next King of Scotland. In May 1303, yet another English invasion of Scotland took place. King Edward occupied Edinburgh and reconquered most of Scotland without facing any serious opposition due to the internal divisions of his enemies. After campaigning in the Highlands, the English were finally able to force the Scots into surrender. The terms of submission stipulated in February 1303, however, were not accepted by William Wallace, who continued to fight with his followers. During the following months, King Edward took all the necessary steps for a final annexation of Scotland to the Kingdom of England, and on 3 August 1305, Wallace was finally captured and sent to London where he was executed as

Archer with longbow. (*Photo and copyright by Antichi Popoli*)

Archer with *chapel de fer* helmet and padded gambeson. (*Photo and copyright by Antichi Popoli*)

a traitor. The hopes of the Scots now rested on Robert Bruce, who, after having eliminated his Scottish rivals and obtained support from most of the Scottish nobles, finally rebelled against Edward I and was crowned King of Scotland on 25 March 1306.

Bruce assembled a new army and soon launched a new campaign to free his realm of the English presence. At the Battle of Methven on 19 June 1306, a Scottish army was easily crushed by the English and Bruce came close to being captured. Following his defeat, he had to abandon mainland Scotland and could do nothing to save his family from Edward I's cruel revenge: most of his relatives were captured by the English and his three brothers were executed. In February 1307, however, Robert resumed his efforts to liberate Scotland from the English and started gathering men again. Some months later, at the Battle of Loudon Hill, he won a minor victory over the English, after which the number of his followers continued to grow. On 6 July 1307, before he could organize a new campaign against Robert Bruce, Edward I of England died in his camp located just south of the Scottish border, after having developed dysentery. His heir and successor, Edward II, left northern England in late August and was crowned king on 25 February 1308.

Chapter 7

The Reigns of Edward II and Edward III

The young Edward II was not comparable to his father in terms of military capabilities and political vision. Although as Prince of Wales he had fought by Edward I's side several times in Scotland, he never achieved significant results. When his father died, instead of continuing the campaign that had been organized to crush the rebellion of Robert Bruce, he preferred to leave northern England in order to be crowned king. This was a huge mistake, since the Scots – who had been under strong pressure until then – now had the time to raise new forces and to reorganize their existing army. In 1308, in order to deprive the Scots of their main ally and to secure the survival of the English presence in Aquitaine, Edward II married Isabella, the only surviving daughter of the King of France. This union was a very important one politically and had some positive consequences for the stability of England, but this soon started to be threatened by the malcontent spreading among the barons. During the early years of his reign, Edward II gave great responsibilities of government to Piers Gaveston, a noble of Gascon origin who became particularly hated since he exerted a very strong influence over the decisions taken by the king. The barons demanded the removal of Gaveston on several occasions and accused him of robbery, while the clergy was also against him and the Archbishop of Canterbury urged Edward to have his favourite excommunicated by the Pope. Gaveston's prominence in government affairs was used by the English nobles as a pretext to organize their opposition against Edward II. The barons wanted more autonomy and for the king to launch new reforms. Gaveston was temporarily exiled, but the king persuaded the nobles to allow him to return in exchange for political concessions: Edward agreed to limit the powers of the Royal Steward and the Marshal of the Royal Household, and also promised to regulate the crown's powers of purveyance and to repeal the recent legislation dealing with customs. After his return, however, Gaveston did nothing to change his political attitude in order to find a compromise with the barons, instead continuing to arrogantly take all the most important decisions without consulting the aristocrats.

This complex political situation had very negative consequences for Edward II, with all his attempts to raise a new army to invade Scotland failing. The crown was short of money, and the barons suspended the collection of new taxes in order to show their malcontent – without money, it was impossible to organize a new campaign. In addition, at least for the moment, the nobles had no intention to fight for a king whom they perceived as a puppet in the hands of Gaveston. In 1310, the monarch was petitioned by the barons to abandon Gaveston as his personal counsellor and to adopt the advice of twenty-one nobles, known as the 'Ordainers', who would form a new consultative council. Being under strong pressure and being left with no choice in the matter, Edward II accepted. Attempting to restore his status as supreme monarch in the eyes of the nobles, he also assembled a small army and marched into Scotland. He tried to force a pitched battle against Robert Bruce, but Bruce employed elusive tactics that prevented the English from achieving any significant results. By the early part of 1311, Edward II had run out of money and was critically short of supplies, being left with no choice but to leave Scotland. Meanwhile, the Ordainers had drawn up their Ordinances for political reform, which the king had to accept upon his return from the north. The Ordinances of 1311 contained several clauses limiting the monarch's right to go to war or to grant land without parliament's approval, while also introducing a system of control that would monitor the adherence of the crown to the Ordinances. Using the weakness of King Edward to their advantage, the barons obliged him to expel Gaveston from his realm and to deprive him of all his titles. A few months after these events, Edward changed his mind and decided to adopt a new policy against the barons, revoking the Ordinances and recalling Gaveston to England. The nobles responded by assembling their troops under the guidance of the Earl of Lancaster, Edward II's powerful cousin and the most influential of the English aristocrats. The following weeks were extremely chaotic politically, Gaveston being captured by the barons and executed after a short trial. The king, meanwhile, tried to assemble an army to seek his revenge.

After Gaveston's death, however, Edward II understood that there was no sense in starting a new civil war: his favourite counsellor had died and the barons were much stronger than the crown from a military point of view. In addition, the monarch needed the support of the barons in order to fight a new – and possibly decisive – campaign against Robert Bruce in Scotland. As a result of these considerations, the king initiated negotiations with the barons and promised to pardon them for their previous actions in exchange for their backing for a new war against the Scots. In 1313, a final agreement between the Crown and the nobles was found. Meanwhile, Edward also negotiated with the King of France in the hope of settling the long-lasting disputes that divided England and France regarding the status of Aquitaine. These talks, however, produced little of substance.

Having restored – at least temporarily – his position in England, Edward II was finally able to assemble a new army of 20,000 men for the invasion of Scotland.

Archer with longbow. (*Photo and copyright by Confraternita del Leone/Historia Viva*)

The force was intercepted by the Scots and a major pitched battle was fought at Bannockburn on 23 and 24 June 1314, where Robert Bruce's 10,000 soldiers faced an enemy that was better-equipped and much more numerous. The clash began when two brigades of English cavalry encountered a body of Scottish knights and attacked it. Indeed, the Battle of Bannockburn was initiated in a very spontaneous manner since neither side had any idea of their enemy's disposition. The initial cavalry clash was favourable to the Scots, who repulsed the brigades that made up the English advance-guard thanks to the intervention of their own infantry (which was not far from the battlefield, unlike those of the English). On the second day of the battle, Edward reached the Scottish positions with all his forces and deployed them in the regular way. During the night, the English had crossed Bannockburn stream and had established their positions on the plain located beyond it. After an initial English attack was easily repulsed, the Scottish infantry of the schiltrons advanced on the English positions with great determination and slowly pushed back Edward's men. The English commanders tried to deploy their excellent archers on the flanks of the advancing Scots, but a charge by the small unit of Scottish cavalry dispersed the English and

Archer with camail. (*Photo and copyright by Antichi Popoli*)

Crossbowman with *chapel de fer* helmet and padded gambeson. (*Photo and copyright by Confraternita del Leone/Historia Viva*)

Detail of a mask helmet. (*Photo and copyright by Confraternita del Leone/Historia Viva*)

Welsh bowmen before they could fire their arrows on the schiltrons. Robert Bruce now had the upper hand, the English cavalry being hemmed in against the Bannockburn stream with no space to manoeuvre. Unable to hold their formation, the English knights broke ranks and fled from the battlefield. The Battle of Bannockburn was a disaster for Edward II and sealed the independence of Scotland, under the guidance of Robert Bruce, who occupied several castles that were still in English hands and exchanged captured enemy nobles for female members of his family who had been imprisoned by Edward I.

Following Bannockburn, Robert Bruce decided to expand his war against England by sending an army under the command of his younger brother, Edward, to Ireland. The King of Scotland hoped to expel the English from Ireland and wanted to have his brother crowned as High King of Ireland. The Scots who landed in Ireland could count on the support of various local rulers, but their presence was soon perceived by the Irish – quite correctly – as a foreign invasion. Consequently, after three years of fighting, the Scottish campaign in Ireland ended in complete failure. On 14 October 1318, at the Battle of Faughart, Edward Bruce was defeated and killed by the army of the Lordship of Ireland. The dream of a united Gaelic realm disappeared, but the difficulties experienced by the Kingdom of England remained. The kingdom was ravaged at this time by the so-called 'Great Famine' that was the result of a string of bad harvests. Revenues from the export of wool plummeted and the price of food rose, causing the death of thousands of English peasants. Most of the population perceived the defeat of Bannockburn and the Great Famine as punishments from God, and complaints about Edward II's rule thus multiplied across the realm since he was considered to be responsible for his country's misfortunes. In order to survive on his throne, the king formed a strong political alliance with the noble family of the Despensers, whose members became his favourites and were appointed to important positions in the royal government. The ascendancy of the Despensers was greatly opposed by the other English barons, who started to organize themselves for a new civil war. The Despensers, meanwhile, became the most powerful of the Marcher Lords.

In early 1321, the Earl of Lancaster mobilized the baronial forces in the Welsh Marches, and some months later the civil conflict known as the Despenser War broke out. The rebellious barons were able to seize the lands of the Despensers in the Welsh Marches very rapidly despite the opposition of the king, and thus forced Edward II to send into exile all the members of the powerful family. Fearing that he might be deposed, especially after the rebels occupied also the city of London, Edward II had no choice but to cede, but he soon started to plan his revenge. After having created internal divisions among his opponents, the monarch recalled the Despensers from exile and assembled a royalist army with which he advanced into the Welsh Marches. Edward was able to obtain a local and easy victory over the Marcher Lords who opposed his rule, and then moved against the Earl of Lancaster, who had assembled a rebel army in northern England. The squabbling among the anti-royalist forces had severely weakened them, so the Earl of Lancaster could now count only on a modest number of troops. As a result, the king's cousin was defeated and captured by Edward II's men at the Battle of Boroughbridge. The king showed no mercy to his relative, who was found guilty of treason and executed. The Despenser War of 1321–1322, against all odds, was a success for Edward II and his favourite noble family. Many titles and lands of the barons who had rebelled against the king were confiscated and assigned to the Despensers, who became increasingly powerful. Thanks to the new fines and confiscations, the crown could restore its financial situation. In addition, Edward was able to permanently revoke the Ordinances of 1311. At this point, with England in his hands, the king decided to resume hostilities against Scotland and assembled a new army of 23,000 soldiers. He rapidly invaded the lands of Robert Bruce, but the Scottish monarch avoided an open battle with the numerically superior English forces. After several months of indecisive campaigning, the English troops ran out of food and Edward was forced to retreat south of the border without having achieved any important results. The failure of this latest Scottish campaign gave the barons another opportunity to reorganize themselves, since by now most of them were convinced that the only way to save the realm was to depose Edward.

In 1324, Edward was involved in a continental conflict against France known as the War of Saint-Sardos. Charles IV, the new French monarch since 1322, was much more aggressive towards Gascony than his predecessor. In 1323, the French king demanded permission for his officials to carry out his royal orders in Gascon territory; this was a first step towards the annexation of Gascony to France, and was totally unacceptable for the English. After some preliminary border skirmishing, Charles IV was ready to invade Gascony by the beginning of 1324. Edward II had just 4,500 knights and foot soldiers on the continent, while the French assembled an army of 7,000 men. In retaliation for the French attack, the King of England ordered the arrest of all French subjects who lived in England and seized all the English lands of his wife Isabella (who was Charles IV's sister). An English army of some 11,000 men was rapidly sent to the threatened territories, but Edward II had no intention of fighting a long war against France. Consequently, he started negotiating with Charles IV in order to find a solution to the conflict. As part of the talks, Edward was required to send Isabella to Paris in 1325 as a diplomatic envoy. The Queen of England was able to find a compromise with which to end the hostilities, but this was extremely favourable for her brother, Charles IV: Edward would have been required to pay homage in person to the King of France in order to retain possession of Gascony. The King of England accepted the proposed terms but gave Gascony to his young son and heir, Edward (the future Edward III), so that it would be the Prince of Wales to offer homage to Charles in Paris. Edward II was thus able to avoid a major international humiliation, but events then took an unexpected turn: his wife

Detail of a camail. (*Photo and copyright by Confraternita del Leone/Historia Viva*)

Detail of a kite shield. (*Photo and copyright by Confraternita del Leone/Historia Viva*)

decided to remain in France, where she was involved in a relationship with one of her husband's exiled opponents, Roger Mortimer, one of the most important Marcher Lords who had been removed by the Despensers. Edward II's opponents soon began to gather around Isabella and Roger in Paris.

The rebel couple, with the covert assistance of Charles IV, concluded an important military alliance with William I, Count of Hainaut, who agreed to marry his daughter, Philippa, to the future Edward III (who had remained in France with his mother) and provided Roger Mortimer with a large fleet with which he could invade England. Soon after the marriage between Prince Edward and Philippa of Hainaut, Isabella and Roger began organizing their invasion of England. During August and September 1326, Edward II mobilized all the forces that were available to him and deployed his warships in the major ports in order to prevent an enemy landing. He also sent a raiding force with 1,600 men across the English Channel to perform a diversionary attack against Normandy. He could count on the support of the Despensers, but most of the other English barons were against him: the great majority of the nobles were ready to revolt against his rule and were just waiting for the right moment to unite their resources. On 24 September, Prince Edward, Isabella of France and Roger Mortimer landed in Suffolk at the head of a small military force, without meeting any resistance. They were soon joined by an increasing number of barons, who rose up in revolt against King Edward, who meanwhile had to face an uprising by London's population and was forced to abandon his capital. He hoped to reach Wales, where he was sure that the Dispensers would be able to raise a new royal army. However, it soon became apparent that the king faced imminent defeat. The Church and the royal administration abandoned him and changed sides, while the number of barons supporting Prince Edward kept growing. The king then tried to flee to Ireland with his remaining followers, but was captured in Wales and escorted back to England. Isabella and Roger Mortimer took revenge on the former regime and practically destroyed the Dispensers. New officials were nominated across the realm, and the crown's government came under their direct control. All the barons agreed on one point: Edward II had to be deposed. At that time, however, there was no established procedure for legally removing a King of England from his throne. Adam Orleton, the Bishop of Hereford, made a series of public allegations about Edward II's conduct as a monarch, and in January 1327 a parliament convened at Westminster in order to decide the future of the king. Most of the English population, especially the crowds of London, were in favour of Prince Edward's ascendancy to the throne, and thus the barons agreed that Edward II must be replaced by his son. The king was officially accused of incompetence, and delegates were sent to convince him to abdicate. The monarch, in tears, finally agreed in order to permit the coronation of his son. On 21 January 1327, Edward II ceased to be the King of England, and on 2 February that year, Edward III was crowned in Westminster.

Fearing that the former king could be freed by some of his remaining supporters, Roger Mortimer moved Edward II to the castle of Berkeley in Gloucestershire, where on 21 September 1327 he died, having probably been murdered on the orders of the new regime. The rule of Roger Mortimer and Isabella over England, however, did not last long after Edward II's death. Neither of them were particularly loved by the English, since most of the common people considered Edward III their only legitimate leader. The couple's popularity was also greatly damaged by the signing of the Treaty of Northampton between England and Scotland, which recognized the full independence of Scotland and Robert Bruce's legitimacy as a king. For the moment, the English crown had renounced its expansionist ambitions over Scotland. Edward III slowly started to limit the personal power of Mortimer in order to begin ruling his realm as an autonomous monarch. In 1330, he ordered the arrest of the powerful aristocrat, who was accused of treason and executed. Isabella of France was spared by her son, but rapidly lost her previous political prominence. Edward III was an intelligent young man and had great ambitions for his kingdom, although he had to rebuild the institutions of his realm practically from scratch and had to pacify large portions of the country. The monarch restored order in Wales and stabilized the political situation in Ireland, while starting to organize his future revenge on Scotland. Gradually, and with many difficulties, the previous prosperity of England was restored, together with the barons' trust in their king.

Edward III was not satisfied with the peace agreement that had been made in his name with Scotland, but for the moment had no intention of resuming hostilities against the Scots. A group of leading English nobles who had lost their lands in Scotland due to the Treaty of Northampton, however, soon started to plot behind the back of the king in order to provoke the outbreak of a new Anglo-Scottish conflict. These barons, known as the 'Disinherited', planned an invasion of Scotland without the official permission of the king and obtained a great victory at the Battle of Dupplin Moor in August 1331. In 1329, Robert Bruce had died, leaving his 4-year-old son David II on the throne of Scotland. The rule of the infant monarch was not accepted by all the Scottish nobles who had opposed his father, and most notably by Edward Balliol, son of John Balliol, who had been King of Scotland before Robert Bruce. The Disinherited soon started to support Edward Balliol, in exchange for the promise of being given back their lands once the supporters of David II were defeated. The decisive clash between the two Scottish factions took place at Dupplin Moor, which ended in victory for Balliol and his English supporters, who made up a good portion of the army that invaded Scotland. A few weeks after the clash, Edward Balliol was

Detail of a triangular shield. (*Photo and copyright by Sirotci*)

crowned King of Scotland. Soon after advancing into his new realm, however, he was ambushed and defeated by the supporters of the Bruce family, and was forced to return to England. The invasion of Scotland organized by the Disinherited without the support of Henry III had ended in complete failure. King Edward III thus found himself involved in a new Scottish war that had not been initiated by him. This began in 1333 and lasted for several years, being known as the Second War of Scottish Independence (the First War of Scottish Independence had been that fought by Edward I).

While these events took place in the British Isles, the political situation also started to change in continental Europe. There was a new monarch on the French throne, Philip VI, who was determined to annex Aquitaine to his realm. In 1337, the French king confiscated the English territorial possessions on the continent and sent an army to occupy them, and after a very short campaign, only Gascony remained in Edward III's hands. At this point, seeing that war with France was inevitable, King Edward refused to seek a peaceful resolution to the crisis and responded to the French moves by laying claim to the crown of France as the grandson of Philip IV. The French nobles, however, considered Edward's claims illegitimate and continued to support Philip VI, who was the nephew of Philip IV. As a result of these events, a new conflict between England and France began; this, however, would only be ended in 1453. The Hundred Years' War had begun. During 1340, several cities in Flanders recognized Edward III as the legitimate King of France, and he officially added the French Royal Arms to his personal heraldry. A struggle initiated over possession of the last remnants of the former Angevin Empire was rapidly transforming itself into a large-scale European war, at the end of which both England and France would

Detail of a knight's sword. (*Photo and copyright by Sirotci*)

emerge as the modern nations that they are today. The first phase of the Plantagenets' long history was over. In less than two centuries, they had been able to transform England into the dominant power of the British Isles and into one of the most important nations of Europe. These results had been achieved through a series of devastating conflicts, fought across a large geographical area. A new military power had been born.

Chapter 8

Organization and Equipment of the Plantagenet Military Forces and of their Enemies

In this concluding chapter we will try to describe the composition of the Plantagenet military forces and those of their opponents in the British Isles. In doing so, we will also provide details on the equipment employed by the various contingents of the armies. The analysis will be divided into five parts, each of which will be dedicated to a different group of military units: the first will cover the troops of the Kingdom of England, the second those recruited by the Plantagenets on the continent (French troops and mercenaries), the third those of Wales, the fourth those of Scotland and the fifth those of Ireland. The chapter is illustrated with several reproductions of magnificent miniatures from the *Morgan Bible*. The latter, more precisely the Ms M.638 of The Pierpont Morgan Library (New York), is a unique illuminated manuscript produced around the middle of the thirteenth century in northern France. The *Morgan Bible* consists of forty-six surviving folios (three of which are not preserved in the Morgan Library), illustrated with miniature paintings of events from the *Bible* that are set in the scenery and costumes of thirteenth-century France. Since most of its miniatures depict biblical battles by reproducing dozens of warriors in medieval military equipment, the *Morgan Bible* is a fundamental visual primary source for anyone interested in reconstructing the appearance of Western Europe's soldiers during the thirteenth century. The original manuscript contained over 380 scenes and was the result of incredible work by six different medieval artists. The *Morgan Bible* is believed to have been created in Paris around 1240 for Louis IX of France, a great 'crusader king' and champion of the Christian cause during the late crusades. The main reason behind the creation of the *Morgan Bible* – which is also known as the *Crusader Bible* for this reason – was probably an attempt to legitimize Louis' military enterprises by presenting them as a continuation of the holy wars initiated by the biblical Jewish kings. After the death of Louis IX, ownership of the manuscript passed to his brother, Charles of Anjou, who was King of Naples. While the book was in Italy, Latin text was added on the margins of its miniatures (the original manuscript had no scripts). The next known owner of the illuminated bible was Cardinal Bernard Maciejowksi (1548–1608), who studied in Italy and likely gained ownership of the book while there before becoming Bishop of Cracow. In

1604, Maciejowksi gifted the bible to Shah Abbas I of Persia through a delegation. The Persian monarch greatly enjoyed the precious gift and ordered the addition of some Persian inscriptions along the margins of its folios. Due to the peculiar events that characterized its long history, the manuscript is today also known as the *Maciejowski Bible* or the *Shah Abbas Bible*. When the Afghans invaded Persia in 1722, Abbas I's library was sacked; the bible, however, was saved in some way. During the following decades, it was preserved by an unknown Persian Jew, who added Judeo-Persian scripts to it. In 1833, the manuscript was auctioned off for a first time by Sotheby's after having been purchased in Cairo. The bible became the property of the famous collector Sir Thomas Phillipps and – following his death – of his relatives. In 1910, Sotheby's again took charge of auctioning the book, selling it to Pierpont Morgan. Thanks to the love for culture of the *Morgan Bible*'s many owners, today we can still count on a formidable iconographic primary source for reconstructing with great detail the appearance of the Plantagenet military forces. For more information and pictures about the *Morgan Bible*, visit the excellent website dedicated to this precious manuscript by the institution that preserves it (The Morgan Library and Museum): https://www.themorgan.org/collection/Crusader-Bible.

England

With the Norman Conquest of 1066, feudalism was brought to the Kingdom of England, King William parcelling out the lands of his new realm to the barons who had fought under his orders at the Battle of Hastings. According to the latest calculations, around 5,000 knights were 'enfeoffed' – i.e. given a fiefdom – by King William during the first phase of his reign. The English lands were not only given to lay barons, but also to clerical nobles who were 'Princes of the Church'. Each baron – lay or clerical – was required to provide the knights who were under his orders to the king in case of war. According to the *Cartae Baronum* of 1166, a compilation of data detailing the military obligations of all the English nobles, 784 knights out of 5,000 were to be provided by clerical barons. Over time, the military system based on sub-infeudation – i.e. the division of the barons' major fiefdoms into minor ones given to knights – became increasingly complex. An important military document dated 1181 (the so-called 'Assize of Arms') prescribed that when the number of knights sub-infeudated within his fiefdom fell short of the knight-service owed to the monarch, a single feudal tenant should maintain sufficient items to equip some knights comprising his personal household in order to make up the difference. Most of the English nobles had personal households consisting of loyal knights who provided military service in exchange for money rather than land. These retines of professional soldiers could consist of just a few individuals, but also of larger contingents, depending on the wealth of the baron paying them. The compulsory military service based on the feudal military structure – known as *servitium debitum* – could last for a maximum of sixty days (later reduced to forty) after mobilization. Initially, the mobilized feudal knights could also be sent to fight overseas to protect the Plantagenet territorial possessions in France, but since John Lackland's reign, most of the English *milites* refused to serve outside the British Isles.

Some major nobles were granted what was known as 'money fief', i.e. they were not required to send their knights to the king in case of war but had to provide a fixed sum of money with which the monarch could recruit mercenary soldiers. This system, however, was never particularly popular in the Plantagenet domains. Feudal military mobilization usually caused malcontent among the barons of the realm, who were more interested in pursuing their own personal interests than those of the monarchy. As a result, after 1157, the Plantagenet kings attempted to introduce a new form of 'partial mobilization' that was based on a quota system. According to this, the monarch was to summon only a portion – one third – of those knights owing feudal military service, and call upon those remaining at home to support the mobilized *milites* economically through the scutage system. The latter was based on a simple principle: if exempted from his military duties, each vassal was to pay a certain sum of money that was to be used for buying and maintaining the personal military equipment of those vassals who had been mobilized. By the end of King John's reign, this system of partial mobilization was no longer in use since it had failed to reach its objectives. The knights holding a fiefdom, however, were not the only professional soldiers who could be called to serve by a Plantagenet king. There were also tenants of an inferior social status, who were known as sergeants. These, despite not being nobles, had been given a land property by the monarchy in exchange for their military services. Originally, the sergeants were required to serve as heavy infantrymen, since they did not have the economic resources to maintain a horse. Over time, however, many of them became rich enough to equip themselves exactly like the noble *milites*. It should be noted, however, that the number of sergeants living in the Kingdom of England always remained quite small – especially if compared with their equivalents serving under the King of France.

Cavalry was not the only component of the Plantagenet armies, which also included sizeable contingents of infantry. After the Norman Conquest of England, the old *fyrd* military system created by the Saxons a few centuries before was not terminated. According to the *fyrd*, each able-bodied free man aged from 16–60 and living in any shire of the Kingdom of England could be called to serve by his overlord in case of war. Those individuals who refused military service were subject to fines

Miniature from the folio 24 *recto* of the *Morgan Bible*, depicting a king and his most important vassals at court. The feudal military system of the Plantagenet Empire was based on the loyalty of the nobles towards their monarch, and thus was greatly influenced by the political attitude of the barons.

or the loss of their properties. A commoner, for example, was to pay a fine of 30 shillings if he neglected compulsory military service. Service in the *fyrd* was usually of short duration and had practically no costs for the royal authorities, since the members of this general levy were expected to provide their own arms and provisions and were not paid by the monarch for their military services. Originally, the *fyrd* was mobilized and organized on a local basis, according to the tribal subdivisions of the various communities, but with the arrival of feudalism, it started to be managed

Miniature from the folio 32 *verso* of the *Morgan Bible*, representing a knight (right) with his squire (left). The knight has full armour and is travelling with his courser, a strong horse of good quality, inferior to the destrier employed in battle but superior to the all-purpose rouncey. The squire, wearing a *chapel de fer*, is transporting the spear of his lord.

by the feudal lords. Each knight could now mobilize a certain number of peasants who lived and worked on his land properties in order to form a small retinue of poorly equipped infantry. In case of large-scale foreign invasions, it was the king's responsibility to call up for the 'national *fyrd*' that was made up of all the able-bodied men of his realm. Conditions of service for the national *fyrd* (also known as the 'great *fyrd*') and for the more common 'shire *fyrd*' were quite different, since in most cases the English commoners were not particularly happy about the idea of serving far from their homes for long periods of time. Most of the English freemen were peasants, who spent their lives working in the fields and following the natural cycles. Consequently, on most occasions, service in the great *fyrd* could last only for very limited periods of time – sixty days, later reduced to forty – and the king had to pay his freemen if any additional period of service was needed. The three most important military documents of the early Plantagenet period – the 1181 Assize of Arms, the 1242 Assize and the 1285 Statute of Winchester – all confirmed the existence of the feudal infantry levy. Since the late Saxon period, a quota system of mobilization also existed inside the *fyrd*; on most occasions, only one freeman from each five hides of land was required to join the national *fyrd* when it was mobilized for a campaign. The selected individual was expected to be equipped with spear and shield; in addition, he was expected to have provisions for two months and to receive a wage of 4 shillings, both of which were provided by the other men living on the five hides of land from which he was levied. The Norman kings abolished payments for the members of the *fyrd*, since feudal military service was considered to be a duty for each peasant. During the late twelfth century, however, the Plantagenets reintroduced them for when the peasant infantrymen were not serving abroad.

During the late Saxon period, a new social class of lesser noblemen, the *thegns*, had emerged from the rural communities and had started to hold estates which averaged five hides in size. These minor landowners, after the Norman Conquest, were mostly transformed into sergeants, who were frequently employed by knights as the commanders of their feudal infantry retinues. It should be noted, however, that the smallest contingents of peasant foot soldiers could be commanded by parish priests, while the largest ones were usually commanded by the local sheriffs. The sheriffs, introduced in England by the Normans, were royal officials responsible for keeping peace in the various shires and for arranging the annual shire payment owed to the king. During the Plantagenet period, the Kingdom of England did not have large urban centres and thus did not see the development of significant urban militias, differently from what happened in the Kingdom of France. Only London could mobilize a certain number of well-equipped infantrymen (around 6,000) who – unlike their equivalents of the feudal levy – were mostly craftsmen and merchants.

Miniature from the folio 41 *recto* of the *Morgan Bible*, showing a battle of knights. None of the figures have heraldic elements reproduced on their surcoats, but all are wearing chainmail hauberks. Most of the knights have great helms, while some have simpler conical helmets with or without nasal. The triangular shield of the king on the left has metal reinforcements on its external surface. Offensive weapons include spears, swords, axes and maces.

Miniature from the *folio 39* recto of the *Morgan Bible*, depicting a clash of knights. Several of the helmets are painted with bright colours, and the caparisons of the horses – like the surcoats of the *milites* – are in a single plain colour.

The Assize of Arms of 1181, a document promulgated by Henry II and detailing the kind of personal equipment that every knight and feudal infantryman had to carry in war, divided the commoners into three military categories according to their economic capabilities: those possessing at least 16 marks of chattels or rents – like the richest sergeants – were to equip themselves as knights with full panoply; those with at least 10 marks of chattels or rents – like the poorest sergeants – were to equip themselves as heavy infantry with helmet, hauberk of chainmail and spear; those possessing less than 10 marks of chattels or rents were to equip themselves with helmet, quilted gambeson and spear. Shields, being defensive weapons, were not mentioned in the document, but were carried by all soldiers. Curiously, Henry II also promulgated an Assize of Arms for his French territorial domains in 1181, but this prescribed different panoplies for the foot troops belonging to the second and third category. The soldiers of the second category were to have helmet, hauberk of chainmail, spear and sword; while those of the third category were to have helmet, quilted gambeson, spear and sword or bow and arrows. These differences are quite interesting, since they show two things: first, that most of the English commoners were too poor to own a sword; second, that the longbow was not yet a popular alternative to the standard infantry spear. Henry III's Assize of 1242 modified the panoply required for each category of freemen. Members of the first were to have helmet, hauberk of chainmail, spear, sword and knife; those of the second were to have helmet, quilted gambeson, spear, sword and knife; and members of the third could have bow and arrows, sword and knife or a single 'peasant weapon' (like a falchion or a gisarme). The most important innovation was the introduction of the bow as an alternative to the standard infantry weapons used by the third category.

Under Edward I, the nature of the English military forces changed considerably. First of all, knights and peasant infantrymen recruited according to the feudal system rapidly became only a secondary component of the English armies. They were replaced by professional soldiers who served for money and without limitations of time and space (something that had always hampered the expansionist campaigns of the earlier Plantagenet kings). The personal household of the monarch, known as the *familia regis*, had previously consisted of just a few knights acting as the personal bodyguard of the king, but under Edward I it was greatly expanded and came to comprise a few hundred knights and mounted sergeants who served for money and responded only to the monarch. These were usually organized into 'constabularies' that each had an average strength of 100 *milites stipendiarii*, or 'paid knights'. The feudal knights, instead, served in small groups of between five and fifteen *milites* each that were the direct heirs of the *conrois* employed in the Norman armies. A variable number of *conrois* could be assembled together to form the larger *batailles*, or 'battles'

– the cavalry divisions deployed for pitched battles. Each knight, whether feudal or mercenary, was usually accompanied on the battlefield by one or two esquires. These played only an auxiliary role and were tasked with managing the three horses owned by each *miles* – the *destrier* or war horse, the *courser* employed for travelling long distances and the *rouncey* used for transporting equipment – but could also fight as light cavalry in case of emergency.

The royal household, in addition to the *milites stipendiarii*, started to include increasing numbers of mercenaries recruited from abroad (mostly from the remaining Plantagenet French possessions in Gascony). The great majority of the Gascon mercenaries were mounted crossbowmen, who moved on horse but fought on foot. The crossbow never became popular in England, due to the ascendancy of the longbow as a national weapon , so the crossbowmen of the English Plantagenet armies were all foreign mercenaries. Edward I, during his conquest of Wales, understood that the local longbowmen could have an enormous combat potential, so soon started to recruit large numbers of them for his military forces. Around 1285, almost two-thirds of the infantrymen serving in the English army were Welsh longbowmen, who had replaced the previous feudal infantry levies. Edward I also sponsored the adoption of the longbow as the standard weapon of the English commoners because he did not want to rely entirely on Welsh archers. The latter were usually organized in constabularies with 100 men each, like their English equivalent. The previous contingents of feudal infantry were usually organized on larger constabularies with 500 men each, but these had mostly disappeared by the beginning of Edward I's reign. A single constabulary with 100 infantrymen was usually divided into five sub-units with twenty soldiers each. Each constabulary was commanded by an officer – equipped as a mounted sergeant – who was known as a *centenar*, while each sub-unit was led by a sort of NCO – equipped as a foot sergeant – who was called a *vintenar*.

The 1285 Statute of Winchester, which remained valid until the end of the period covered in this book, modified the panoply that each category of English soldier was to carry on the battlefield. It divided the English subjects who could be called to serve into six distinct categories, each formulated according to the economic capabilities of its members. The first category included individuals who owned more than £40 of land, who were required to equip themselves as heavy knights; the second category comprised those who owned more than £20 of land, who were to equip themselves as mounted sergeants; the third category included men who owned more than £15 of land, who were required to equip themselves as heavy infantrymen with chainmail hauberk; the fourth category were those who owned more than £10 of land, who were to equip themselves as medium infantry with quilted gambeson; the fifth category included men who owned more than £2 of land,

Miniature from the folio 34 *recto* of the *Morgan Bible*, representing an army marching out from the walls of a fortified city. The professional foot soldiers following the knights are equipped like the latter and are armed with battle staffs or poleaxes.

who had to equip themselves as longbowmen (with bow, sword and knife); and the sixth category included individuals who owned less than £2 of land, who could arm themselves with a longbow or with whatever 'peasant weapon' they might have. With the enacting of the Statute of Winchester, the standard procedures for mobilization were also changed. In the event of war, the king was to appoint a Commission of Array, made up of experienced knights, usually coming from the royal household, who were tasked with recruiting the necesssary number of soldiers from the various shires and urban centres of the realm and then to assemble them into constabularies. Military service was performed at the individual's expense if conducted within the boundaries of his country, and at the king's expense if outside the kingdom. During the early years of the fourteenth century, the Plantagenet monarchs started recruiting military contingents in a new way, according to the 'indenture system'. This worked quite simply: the king stipulated a formal contract with one of his nobles for raising a certain number of soldiers for a precise period of time and in exchange for the payment of a predetermined sum of money. The new system derived its name from

Miniature from the folio 27 *recto* of the *Morgan Bible*, showing a mounted sergeant. Sometimes the sergeants – professional soldiers of great experience – were equipped exactly like the noble *milites* and had a personal squire like in this case. Note the use of a massive *chapel de fer*, as well as of metal plates acting as greaves.

the fact that such a contract had an indented edge that, in order to prevent forgery, had to match perfectly with the corresponding indents on the top or bottom edge of the king's counterfoil. The creation of the indenture system was the result of the feudal military organization's gradual collapse: during the early Plantagenet period, the English barons had been obliged to send their knights to the king in the case of war, while by the beginning of the late Plantagenet era, the monarch had to pay his nobles in exchange for their military services exactly as if they were mercenary warlords.

During the period known as The Anarchy, the general appearance of English heavy knights was not so different from that of the Norman ones who had followed William the Conqueror in 1066. The *milites* were still mainly protected by a hauberk,

Miniature from the folio 28 *verso* of the *Morgan Bible*, depicting the duel between David and Goliath. The former is represented as a peasant slinger of the feudal levy, armed only with a sling; the latter is equipped as a sergeant, with *chapel de fer* and padded poleyn knee protectors.

omnies um in ca cccceren̄tur. ẏrbiſqȝ ipſa aḣ.adxm.a cēr. nēc t̄ prēdꝛa cꜹ̄uc qu.ım ab aliquo tꜹ̄ꝯꝯe
retur. ẏmus autem filioꝛuȝ iſꝛalel contra precepcum ꝺꜳ aliqm̄ꝺ ex p̄edꝛ.a.tulerat atꝗ̄ occꝺꝺ.ꝛ.

Miniature from the folio 10 *recto* of the *Morgan Bible*, representing a battle taking place in front of the walls of a fortified city. The infantryman with glaive polearm on the left is wearing a padded gambeson painted in red, while the one with poleaxe on the right has a light brown gambeson. Both have a *chapel de fer* helmet.

or shirt of mail, which was made of several thousand interlocking metal rings. The dimensions of each hauberk could vary considerably, since the sleeves could be only to the elbow or have full arm-length. At the bottom, a hauberk generally reached the knees, but could be longer or shorter. Producing this kind of armour was a long and costly process, which only nobles could sustain. Nevertheless, the diffusion of chainmail among knights was practically universal. The chainmail was worn over a padded garment known as a gambeson, which offered additional protection to its wearer. By the middle of the twelfth century, the personal protection of a knight also included other elements made from chainmail, including *chausses* (armour protecting the legs) and gloves. Separate coifs of mail for protection of the head were not yet in use, and the chainmail protecting head and neck was simply part of the hauberk. The standard conical helmet with nasal of the Normans was still very popular, but a semi-spherical version of it with full facial mask was becoming increasingly common. During the late twelfth century, due to the increasing diffusion of the crossbow on European fields of battle, most knights started to abandon their previous helmets with no protection for the face (except for the nasal) and replaced them with new ones having different patterns of facial masks. These masks were fixed and initially gave protection only to the front part of the face, but they later started to have larger dimensions in order to also cover the sides of the face. Consequently, the helmets gradually transformed into full 'great helms' providing complete protection to the head. Regarding shields, there was a progressive transition from the Norman kite shield to the new triangular shield that was used for most of the Middle Ages. The main offensive weapons of the knights were the spear and the long sword. The adoption of closed helmets ended any possibility of recognizing the identity of a knight on the field of battle; to solve this problem, heraldry saw a rapid growth as each noble family started to develop a distinctive emblem. This was initially painted only on the shield of each knight, but was later also reproduced on a new piece of garment that came into use: the surcoat. This was worn over the hauberk and initially had no embroidered decoration. Over the following decades, the heraldic display of each knight was completed by the presence of a coloured crest that was placed on top of the helmet. Until 1200, war horses were not protected by any specific piece of equipment, but during the early thirteenth century, the widespread diffusion of the crossbow led to the creation of new defensive elements specifically designed for horses that could be made from quilted material or chainmail. Initially, these protected only the head, but were later improved in order to protect the entire body of the horse.

The second half of the thirteenth century saw the decisive development of plate armour, which started to be worn in combination with the traditional hauberks. This important evolution, like several others, was encouraged by the increasing use and effectiveness of the crossbow. Initially, plate armour was mostly made of *cuir bouilli* (boiled leather) and consisted of discs protecting the shoulders and the knees. However, leather soon started to be substituted by metal, and new pieces of plate armour – such as greaves – came into use. The protection of the head and neck, meanwhile, had been improved thanks to the introduction of a hood made of chainmail – known as a camail – that was separate from the hauberk. The torso of the *milites* started to be protected by a robust coat of plates, formed by many small and flat pieces of iron that were all riveted together inside a thick fabric garment buckled at the back. During this same period, most of the knights began using maces or axes as an alternative secondary weapon to the long sword. By the beginning of the fourteenth century, the hauberk of each knight was usually supplemented by a series of additional defensive elements of often richly decorated plate armour: *vambraces, cuisses, gauntlets, poleyns* and *sabatons*. Meanwhile, a new form of open helmet, known as *chapel de fer*, had become popular among the *milites*. This wide-brimmed helmet was initially designed for the infantry, but since it was much more comfortable to

Miniature from the folio 3 *verso* of the *Morgan Bible*, showing a surprise attack launched against a military encampment. The infantrymen on the right have been surprised by their enemies and are still trying to put on their padded gambesons or chainmail hauberks; the attackers on the left, two of which have padded infulae for protection of the head, are armed with axe and fauchard. The latter was a deadly infantry weapon consisting of a scythe-like blade having a point at the top and a hook at the back (specifically designed to unhorse knights).

wear than the various models of great helm, the *chapel de fer* was also adopted by many knights. Sergeants were equipped more or less like knights, but their armour was usually lighter than that of the *milites*; after the knights adopted plate armour, for example, most of the sergeants continued to wear simple hauberks.

As we have seen from analysis of the most important military documents enacted by the Plantagenet monarchs, the poorest feudal infantrymen had no military equipment to speak of: they went to war with their ordinary clothes and were mostly armed with their agricultural tools. The more fortunate of them had a padded gambeson and a simple helmet (usually of conical shape, later replaced by the wide-brimmed *chapel de fer*). The foot sergeants and the mercenary infantrymen from the continent, covered more extensively below, were much better equipped than the peasant levies: they all had helmets and frequently wore a full chainmail over their gambeson. Some of them even had *chausses*, while almost all were armed with long pikes that had to be used with both hands. The quilted gambeson – the armour of the poors – was also quite popular among the archers and crossbowmen. It was usually made of linen or

Miniature from the folio 18 *recto* of the *Morgan Bible*, depicting the standard clothes worn by peasants during the thirteenth century. These were used with no alterations by the feudal infantrymen mobilized for war, who had a very humble appearance. The white infulae and the wicker wide-brimmed hats were quite popular, as well as the pants covering the legs. The second figure from the right is wearing his white working breeches without the coloured pants.

wool, with the stuffing being obtained from various materials such as scrap cloth or horse hair. Quilted hoods for protection of the head were usually worn together with the gambeson. During the thirteenth century, the gambeson was improved with the addition of new components like quilted collars or quilted gloves. Many of the feudal infantrymen did not have a shield, although the mercenary foot soldiers were usually equipped with kite or triangular shields. The archers tended to carry a sword and a knife in addition to the longbow; sometimes they could also have a small round shield, but they wore no armour or had only a light gambeson. Crossbowmen often had hauberks or gambesons, worn together with a *chapel de fer*. Since their main weapon had to be used with both hands, they had no shields and thus were usually deployed behind a line of *pavisiers* – specialized infantrymen equipped with a large,

Miniature from the folio 43 *verso* of the *Morgan Bible*, representing an army besieging a walled city. On the left it is possible to see a traction trebuchet manned by feudal levies, one of the most effective siege weapons of the Middle Ages.

flat shield known as a *pavise*. The latter, however, only became popular in England during the Hundred Years' War.

During the Plantagenet period, the English navy also underwent significant development, largely because control of the English Channel was vital for connecting the Plantagenet domains in the British Isles with those located in France. The best warships of the medieval English navy were provided to the Plantagenet monarchs by the Cinque Ports: Hastings, New Romney, Hythe, Dover and Sandwich. These five coastal centres located on the English Channel enjoyed a series of privileges in exchange for the military contribution that they gave to the Plantagenets. In 1155, a Royal Charter of Henry II established that the Cinque Ports had to maintain fifty-seven vessels ready for 'royal service', for fifteen days every year in time of peace and for longer periods in the event of war. In exchange, the Cinque Ports enjoyed the following privileges: exemption from royal taxes, permission to levy tolls and permission to administer local justice autonomously. Under John Lackland, the Cinque Ports became flourishing commercial centres and the main bases of the

Miniature from the folio 23 *verso* of the *Morgan Bible*, showing the culminating moment of a siege. The attackers are employing a trebuchet, while the defenders include an archer armed with longbow and equipped with a simple skull helmet (*cervelière*).

English vavy. Edward I, understanding the importance of these coastal settlements for his military plans, granted their citizens the right to bring goods into his kingdom without paying import duties. When a new war began, it was common practice for the royal authorities to supplement the warships provided by the Cinque Ports with impressed merchant vessels, the crews of which were paid for their services and were mostly tasked with transporting military contingents. The owners of the impressed ships, however, received no compensation from the royal government. Additional naval resources were provided by the small private fleet of the monarch, which was based at the Tower of London and near London Bridge. By 1330, these 'King's Ships' consisted of forty vessels, which were used for patrolling or escort duties.

French troops and mercenaries

The Norman army that invaded England in 1066 included a sizeable number of mercenaries from northern France, and King William continued to recruit professional soldiers on the continent – from the French regions of Brittany, Anjou and Maine – for most of his reign. During the Anarchy period, both King Stephen and Empress Matilda had sizeable mercenary contingents under their command.

These mostly consisted of Welsh light infantrymen and Brabançon/Flemish heavy infantrymen. The latter were particularly appreciated, since they were the only foot soldiers of Western Europe who could resist a cavalry charge on the open field thanks to their excellent personal equipment. A standard Brabançon/Flemish infantryman was a pikeman equipped with helmet and chainmail as well as a shield. The pikes (*geldons*) of such professional soldiers, who were extremely loyal to their employers if paid regularly, were 10–12ft long and could cause serious harm to a heavy knight from a distance. Empress Matilda, who had ruled the Holy Roman Empire for several years, knew very well the excellent combat capabilities of the Brabançon/Flemish mercenary infantry, who continued to be employed in England by Henry II and Richard the Lionheart. The mercenary Welsh light infantry, equipped as fast-moving spearmen or as longbowmen, were mostly employed by the early Plantagenets to fight in France. After the Battle of Bouvines and the signing of the Magna Carta, the number of foreign mercenaries used by the English kings declined considerably because the powerful barons considered the contingents of professional soldiers as a potential menace to their freedom. For their French military campaigns, however, the Plantagenet monarchs continued to recruit large numbers of local mercenaries (notably Gascon crossbowmen). Since the English knights and feudal levies were always reluctant to serve overseas, the Plantagenet armies fighting in France mostly consisted of two categories of troops: local knights and feudal levies from the French regions that were under Plantagenet control, and mercenaries from various areas of France or more distant regions (such as Wales or Flanders). After parts of Ireland were occupied by the English, the Plantagenet forces started to include some contingents of Irish auxiliaries. These consisted of feudal levies made up of light infantrymen, who were recruited by the Anglo-Irish lords who owned fiefdoms in the newly conquered areas of Ireland. Initially, the feudal contingents recruited by the Plantagenets in their French territorial possessions were of excellent quality and quite large, especially those coming from Normandy. These troops, however, could not be employed outside their home territories, and usually refused to serve for long periods of time. They were organized and equipped very similarly to their English equivalents. It should be noted, however, that the French infantry in Plantagenet service included sizeable numbers of well-armed urban militiamen as well as of well-trained crossbowmen. After most of the Plantagenet domains in France were lost during King John's reign, only Gascony remained under English control. The military forces of this region included feudal contingents raised by the most prominent local nobles as well as urban militiamen from the major Gascon cities such as Bordeaux.

Wales

At the beginning of the eleventh century, the territory of present-day Wales was fragmented into a series of small princedoms which were constantly at war against each other. These petty states were the direct heirs of some extremely old tribal traditions, which had changed very little during the centuries of Saxon dominance over England. Despite being politically fragmented, the Welsh had been able to preserve their freedom for a long time by repulsing all the Saxon attacks directed against their lands. They thus became famous for their warlike national spirit and were undoubtedly an extremely dangerous enemy for any army that attempted to invade Wales. Geographically, the country is characterized by a very harsh terrain that is not suitable for the battlefield use of large cavalry contingents. The only troop type that could fight in Wales with a high degree of effectiveness was light infantry, so the great majority of Welsh warriors were equipped as highly mobile skirmishers. Those from northern Wales were mostly equipped as spearmen, while those from the south were armed with the deadly longbow. The longbow was the national weapon of Wales during the medieval period and – as we have seen – was adopted by an increasing number of English foot soldiers as their main weapon. Around 1100, the various princedoms of Wales were subdivided into a series of minor territorial entities, having a tribal nature and being known as *cantrefs*, each of which was dominated by a minor warlord or *uchelwr*. All the able-bodied Welsh males over 14 years of age were expected to serve under their warlord during times of war. According to Giraldus Cambrensis' *Description of Wales* (*c*.1193), all Welsh freemen were extremely happy to fight for the defence of their homeland or to raid the territories of their local enemies. Military service was more a right than a duty, and the endemic state of war existing in medieval Wales had greatly improved the combat capabilities of its warriors. They knew their homelands very well and were used to fighting with hit-and-run guerrilla tactics that based their success on high mobility.

The Welsh warriors received no pay for their military service, but could divide among themselves the booty taken from defeated enemies. They were quite reluctant to fight for long periods of time outside the borders of their princedom, and thus external campaigns usually lasted for a maximum of six weeks. Any freeman incapable of providing military service himself had to equip and send another individual in his place. Unfree males were usually conscripted only to perform auxiliary duties like building encampments or transporting materials. Each major Welsh prince had a retinue of professional soldiers under his direct command, collectively known as his *teulu*, or family. They were often relatives of the warlord, being given sustenance and land by the prince in exchange for their military services. Members of the *teulu* were the only Welsh warriors to have horses, but they usually dismounted to fight and thus did not perform as true cavalry. In most cases, the fighting family of a major prince numbered around 120 professional warriors, who were all *uchelwyr* (plural for *uchelwr*). These were equipped with helmet and chainmail similarly to the contemporary English knights, while the Welsh commoners fighting as spearmen or archers wore no personal protection and carried only their offensive weapons in combat. Welsh spears were not particularly long, since they tended to be used as throwing javelins. Welsh shields were round, and were carried by all the *uchelwyr* and some of the spearmen. Sometimes a Welsh prince could enlarge his *teulu* by recruiting foreign mercenaries, who were mostly Irishmen or warriors of the Viking communities still existing in Ireland (mainly coming from Dublin). The Norman kings of England, having been unable to conquer Wales, created a series of highly autonomous baronies on the border that divided Welsh lands from those of the English. These baronies, known as the Welsh Marches, were assigned to the most warlike Norman nobles, who were tasked with defending the frontier as well as with penetrating – slowly

Miniature from the folio 42 *recto* of the *Morgan Bible*, depicting the storming of a fortified city's walls. One attacker and one defender are armed with stirrup crossbows. On the extreme right it is possible to see a slinger from the feudal levy with wide-brimmed hat and small round shield.

but steadily – into Wales. The barons of the Welsh Marches continued to be the most powerful warlords of England under the Plantagenets, enjoying a series of military privileges: for example, they could build castles and mobilize troops without asking for the formal permission of the monarch. The military forces of the Marcher Lords were made up of the most battle-hardened veterans of England and played a prominent role during the early campaigns that were fought by the Plantagenets in Ireland. They included large numbers of Welsh longbowmen from the late eleventh century onwards, which made them quite different from the contingents of the other English barons. Two of the most prominent Marcher Lords, Gilbert de Clare and his son Richard, were nicknamed Strongbow, probably because their military successes were based on extensive use of Welsh longbowmen.

Scotland

By the time of the Norman conquest of England, the territory of Scotland had already been unified as the Kingdom of Alba, which only became known as the Kingdom of Scotland after the outbreak of the Scottish Independence Wars caused by the dynastic crisis of 1286. In medieval Scotland, all the able-bodied males aged between 16 and 60 could be called to serve in the *exercitus Scoticanus*, or 'common army', which included freemen (most of whom were farmers owning small land properties) as well as *neyfs* or unfree men. The latter were not slaves, but individuals who were tied for life to the land where they had been born. The *neyfs* could be sold or given away with the land on which they lived and worked, but were not treated as slaves. Scottish territory was divided into small units of arable land – known as *arachors* – whose inhabitants were usually asked to provide one soldier each in case of mobilization. When needed, however, every free or unfree man owning a cow could be recruited. In each Scottish shire, the infantrymen who made up the *exercitus Scoticanus* were raised by local officials known as *thanes*. The contingents of the various *thanes* were then grouped under the orders of a major chieftain. This kind of traditional Gaelic military organization, which comprised no cavalry, remained unchanged for centuries since the process that saw the introduction of feudalism into Scotland was extremely slow. By the end of the thirteenth century, the Gaelic chieftains of the Lowlands had mostly been transformed into feudal earls by the monarchs of Scotland, but feudalism was still practically non-existent in the Highlands.

The Scottish kings tried to have military households consisting of mercenary English knights, since these had no rivals in Scotland from a tactical point of view. The Scottish nobles, however, always stopped their monarchs' plans by revolting against them when they recruited too many foreign mercenaries. After the Battle of Stirling Bridge, William Wallace tried to introduce some form of conscription by inflicting heavy punishments on those individuals who failed to answer the call to arms, but his innovations were abandoned soon after his death. According to a Statute of Arms issued in 1318, every Scottish layman possessing at least £10 in goods was to serve by equipping himself with helmet and padded gambeson, whereas laymen possessing less than £10 in goods were to equip themselves with just a spear or bow. Once each year, the personal panoply of each potential soldier had to be inspected by royal officials. The few Scottish feudal knights serving during the Plantagenet period were equipped exactly like their English equivalents, but the infantry of the common army were mostly armed as pikemen. They wore short-sleeved hauberks of chainmail or padded gambesons, which were employed together with a simple skull helmet or – from the early fourteenth century – a *chapel de fer*. The latter were usually worn over a padded hood or 'infula', but there were many foot soldiers who used the infula as their only head protection since they were not rich enough to purchase a helmet. The pikes had wooden shafts up to 15ft long and thus had to be handled with both hands, so the Scottish foot soldiers could carry only small round shields made of wooden planks (sometimes reinforced with metal bosses). These were of some use only against enemy arrows fired from a distance. As a secondary weapon, a Scottish infantryman could carry a small axe or a knife. The Scottish pikemen fought in a compact tactical formation known as a schiltron, which was an evolution of the previous – and extremely common – shield wall. Basically, a schiltron was a phalanx-style battle formation, whose main aim was to present an enemy cavalry

Miniature from the folio 24 *verso* of the *Morgan Bible*, representing the looting operations that usually followed the success of a *chevauchée* or raid. On the right it is possible to see some captured infantrymen being carried away together with stolen cattle (the latter was important for the provisioning of the feudal armies on campaign).

charge with a defensive perimeter that the horses would refuse to breach. William Wallace perfected the schiltron formation but did not invent it, since the use of this tactical deployment is attested in Scotland as far back as the eleventh century. The schiltrons could be of two kinds: circular and rectilinear. The first was essentially static, with the soldiers in the front ranks kneeling with their pike butts fixed into the ground, while those in the rear ranks levelled their pikes over their comrades' heads. The result was a thick-set grove of pikes, which could be fortified by driving stakes into the ground in front of the men of the front ranks. These stakes could be linked with ropes. The rectilinear schiltron, meanwhile, was capable of conducting offensive actions and was greatly developed by Robert Bruce, who drilled his men in the use of the pike as an offensive anti-cavalry weapon. For an infantry army like the *exercitus Scoticanus*, employing the schiltrons was the only way to defeat the numerous and effective heavy cavalry of the Plantagenets.

Ireland

Medieval Ireland consisted of several small kingdoms, each of which was based on tribal units singularly known as *tuath* and consisting of several family groups who had lived on the same territory for a long time. The various family groups could be free (the *soer-chele*) or unfree (the *doer-chele*). The first groups were dominant inside their *tuath*, while the second had to accept the decisions taken by the members of the *soer-chele* more or less like vassals. The leading nobles of the *soer-chele* could be kings of three different types: *Ri-tuaithe*, king of one *tuath*; *Rui-ri*, king of more than one *tuath*; or *Ri-ruirech*, monarch of one of the Irish kingdoms. There were also the High Kings, monarchs of one kingdom who temporarily came to exert a direct or indirect influence over some of the other Irish realms. The title of High King was mostly a ceremonial one, since during the medieval period – with the notable exception of Brian Boru – no Irish king was able to unify the whole island under his control or to stop the continuous inter-state wars that ravaged Ireland. In the event of war, all the able-bodied adult males of both the *soer-chele* and *doer-chele* were to follow their *Ri-tuaithe* or *Rui-ri* in battle; the latter, of course, was obliged to serve under his *Ri-ruirech* when required to do so. At the beginning of the eleventh century, the armed forces fielded by a single *tuath* usually consisted of 700 warriors, who were assembled into a *buiden*, or 'band'. Each band consisted of seven 'hundreds' or *cet*. Over time, most of the Irish military units started to consist of 300 warriors, and thus were known as *tricha cet*. There were no precise time limits for military service, but in most cases it was impossible for a king to raise his forces during autumn or spring because those were the periods of the year when his subjects had to work in the fields.

Miniature from the folio 27 *verso* of the *Morgan Bible*, showing the baggage train of a feudal army in the thirteenth century. Carts were used to transport all the equipment of troops, including helmets and chainmail. Mules and donkeys were employed on a large scale, being vital elements of the military logistic system. The infantrymen coming from the feudal levies manned the carts and were tasked with transporting the various materials. Each battle or division of an army had its own distinctive banner, which was also transported on its carts, in order to make them easily recognizable. The foot sergeant in the centre of the scene is very well equipped, with *chapel de fer* and padded gambeson (including a specific protection for the neck), while the standard-bearer on the right is wearing a corectum (leather cuirass for the torso).

The Viking invasions and incursions changed Ireland forever, with the Scandinavian presence on the island becoming a permanent one. A new mixed population emerged from the Irish and Vikings, that of the *Gall-Gael*, or 'Foreign Gaels'. These soon earned a reputation as skilled warriors and started to be employed as mercenaries by the various Irish warlords. Before the arrival of the Scandinavians, the few foreign mercenaries hired by the Irish kings came from Scotland, but over time consistent numbers of *Gall-Gael* professional soldiers started to act as the 'household' of various Irish monarchs.

From the late eleventh century onwards, some elements of the military system described above started to change. The old *buiden* of 700 warriors was gradually replaced by the new *cat mor* of 1,000 warriors as the new basic military unit, although the *cat mor* continued to consist of 'hundreds'. By the time of the Plantagenet invasion, the *tricha cet* had transformed itself into an administrative unit, with each *tuath* starting to be divided into a certain number of 'three hundreds', each of which consisted of three *bailles* or groups of 100 households. In the event of war, each household was to provide one warrior, but general mobilizations could see a single household providing two or three men for military service. The traditional Irish military system, however, began declining after the Plantagenet invasion, since the tribal contingents were usually reluctant to serve far from their homes for long periods. They had been created to conduct rapid inter-tribal campaigns, not long wars fought against foreign invaders who had settled in parts of Ireland. The crisis of the traditional military system corresponded to the increasing importance of foreign mercenaries of mixed Irish-Scandinavian descent. The Irish monarchs started to recruit larger numbers of professional soldiers from the *Gall-Gael* communities living in Ireland. Urban centres that were still inhabited by large Scandinavian groups – like Wexford and Waterford, as well as Dublin – became the main bases of these mercenaries, who fought like Vikings and were known as *Ostmen*. Ruled by hereditary earls, they earned a living fighting as mercenaries or raiding the British Isles as pirates on their agile warships, which were characterized by a distinctive Scandinavian design. By the end of the twelfth century, however, most of the Irish urban centres inhabited by *Gall-Gael* communities had been occupied by the Plantagenets, and thus the Irish kings had to look elsewhere to find new contingents of mercenaries.

The Western Isles (the Hebrides and the Isle of Man) and the western seaboard of Scotland were still inhabited by large Norse-Gael communities, which were the result of encounters between the local population and Vikings that had taken place several decades before. The warriors of these mixed communities, like the Irish *Gall-Gael*, fought in the Viking way and were well known for their combat ferocity. Around 1150, they started to be recruited as mercenaries by the Irish kings, initiating a practice that would last until the early seventeenth century. By 1250, they started to be called *galloglass* ('foreign warriors') and had become a permanent component of each Irish monarch's personal household. From the early fourteenth century, the Norse-Scottish mercenaries were considered to be the elite of the Irish armies, being better trained and better equipped than the ordinary Irish tribal warriors. The *galloglass* were organized into *corughadhs*, or 'companies', with 100–160 men apiece, and each of them had a senior servant who performed auxiliary duties (such as transporting the personal equipment of the warrior) as well as a junior servant who cooked. The basic unit formed by one warrior, one senior servant and one junior servant was known as a *spar*. The latter term derived from the word *sparth*, which was used to indicate the deadly double-handed axe carried by each *galloglass*. With the ascendancy of the *galloglass*, the standard Irish light infantrymen in a tribal organization started to be known as *kerns*. From 1307, the Statute of Winchester was also applied on the

Irish territories of the Plantagenets, so the Anglo-Irish feudal lords could recruit the able-bodied Irish males living on their fiefdoms at times of war. It should be noted, however, that most of the Anglo-Irish troops fighting for the Plantagenets consisted of a few English knights who had settled in Ireland and of larger numbers of *kerns* provided by the Irish warlords who were subjects or allies of the English.

The standard Irish medieval warrior, before the appearance of the *galloglass*, was a light infantryman armed with one short spear and two throwing javelins. Small round shields were quite popular, although helmets were rare to find and armour was non-existent. Only the noble warriors used chainmail and went to the battlefield mounted on horses. All the Irish fighters had a long dagger for close combat known as a *skein*. Until the middle of the thirteenth century, the Irish warriors did not employ bows but only slings. Some of them did later start to arm themselves as archers, but with short bows of a local design and not with the much more effective Welsh longbow. In addition to the few mounted nobles, the small Irish cavalry contingents comprised some light horsemen armed with throwing javelins. According to Giraldus Cambrensis' precious descriptions, the *galloglasses* – from the time of their appearance – were equipped as heavy infantrymen with helmet and hauberk of chainmail. As previously mentioned, the main offensive weapon of these Norse-Scottish mercenaries was the double-handed *sparth* axe.

Bibliography

Ambler, S.T., *The Song of Simon de Montfort: England's First Revolutionary and the Death of Chivalry* (Picador, 2019).

Asbridge, T., *The Greatest Knight: The remarkable life of William Marshal, the Power behind five English Thrones* (Simon & Schuster, 2015).

Barber, R., *Henry II. A Prince amongst Princes* (Penguin, 2015).

Barratt, N., *The Restless Kings: Henry II, his Sons and the Wars for the Plantagenet Crown* (Faber & Faber, 2019).

Bartlett, C., *English Longbowman 1330–1515* (Osprey Publishing, 1995).

Bartlett, R., *England under the Norman and Angevin Kings 1075–1225* (Oxford University Press, 2003).

Bartlett, W.B., *Richard the Lionheart: the Crusader King of England* (Amberley Publishing, 2019).

Cannan F., *Galloglass 1250–1600* (Osprey Publishing, 2010).

Gravett, C., *English Medieval Knight 1200–1300* (Osprey Publishing, 2002).

Gravett, C., *Norman Knight 950–1204* (Osprey Publishing, 1994).

Green, J.A., *Henry I: King of England and Duke of Normandy* (Cambridge University Press, 2009).

Heath I., *Armies of Feudal Europe 1066–1300* (Wargames Research Group, 1989).

Heath I., *Armies of the Dark Ages 600–1066* (Wargames Research Group, 1980).

Heath I., *Armies of the Middle Ages, Volume I* (Wargames Research Group, 1982).

Jones, D., *The Plantagenets: The Warrior Kings and Queens who made England* (Viking, 2013).

Loades, M., *The Longbow* (Osprey Publishing, 2013).

Morris, M., *A Great and Terrible King: Edward I and the forging of Britain* (Pegasus, 2017).

Morris, M., *King John: Treachery, Tyranny and the Road to Magna Carta* (Hutchinson, 2015).

Nicolle, D., *The Normans* (Osprey Publishing, 1987).

Prestwich, M., *Plantagenet England 1225–1360* (Oxford University Press, 2007).

Rothero, C., *The Scottish and Welsh Wars 1250–1400* (Osprey Publishing, 1984).

Spencer, C., *The White Ship: Conquest, Anarchy and the Wrecking of Henry I's Dream* (William Collins, 2020).

Warner, K., *Edward II: The Unconventional King* (Amberley Publishing, 2014).

Weir, A., *Eleanor of Aquitaine: By the Wrath of God, Queen of England* (Vintage, 2008).

The Re-enactors who Contributed to this Book

Confraternita del Leone/Historia Viva

La 'Confraternita del Leone' è un'associazione culturale di ricostruzione storica, con l'obiettivo di studiare, rivivere e divulgare la storia lombarda, con particolare attenzione a quella di Brescia e delle popolazioni che l'hanno abitata nei secoli. Le ricerche dei nostri studiosi spaziano senza limiti nella ricca e complessa storia locale, concentrando l'aspetto rievocativo e didattico sui periodi dal IV al I secolo a.C. in cui furono protagonisti Reti, Celti e Romani, quindi sul secolo VIII dei Longobardi, sull'età dei Comuni e delle Signorie del XII e XIII secolo e infine sul XVII secolo e l'epoca dei Buli sotto la Repubblica di Venezia. La ricerca storica della *Confraternita del Leone* si articola su tre differenti e complementari piattaforme di studio, la cui finalità è raggiungere dei risultati di globalità analitica in grado di estrinsecare degli spaccati storici di corretta filologicità e, ove possibile, di assoluto realismo e scientificità: istituto di ricerca storica, laboratori di archeologia sperimentale e accademia di antiche arti marziali occidentali. Nel partecipare ad eventi storici la *Confraternita del Leone* allestisce un accampamento di circa 500 metri quadrati, dispone di vari antichi mestieri dimostrativi con artigiani all'opera tra cui il fabbro con la forgia, la tessitura a telaio, la macinazione di cereali, l'usbergaro, lo speziale, il cerusico, la zecca, il cambiavalute, il cacciatore, l'arcaio, lo scrivano, l'avvocato e il fabbricante di candele; in battaglia sono schierati arcieri, balestrieri, fanteria, ariete, trabucchi e mantelletti.

Contacts:
E-mail: confraternitadelleone@gmail.com
Website: http://www.confraternitaleone.com/
Facebook: https://www.facebook.com/confraternitadelleone

Sirotci z.s.

Sirotci is a registered living history association focused on the re-enacting of the early fourteenth century. It deals with the reconstruction of the military and everyday life of the inhabitants of the Kingdom of Bohemia between the years 1300 and 1330. Within two noblemen's suites – those of Javornice and Dobeve – we try to reconstruct several layers of medieval society in many aspects. Each fellow of the suite has their own life story, which influences the behaviour of their character. We try to use clothing, objects of daily use, armour and weapons in the correct form we know from period depictions (illuminations, statues) and archaeological finds. We participate in various events, from historical battles, assemblies and tournaments to simple open-air marches.

Contacts:
E-mail: wencacerny@seznam.cz
Website: http://sirotci.cz/
Facebook: https://www.facebook.com/sirotcizs/

Antichi Popoli

L'Associazione Culturale "Antichi Popoli" nasce nel 2002 dalla passione di alcuni ragazzi per la storia e la promozione del patrimonio culturale del territorio. L'associazione attualmente cura la ricostruzione storica di tre periodi: medievale (1289-1325), etrusco (VI-IV sec. a.C.) e celtico (III-I sec. a.C.). Assieme ai suoi anni di esperienza e ricerca, può vantare anche l'iscrizione ad alcuni enti quali l'elenco regionale delle associazioni di rievocazione storica della Regione Toscana e il C.E.R.S. La scelta del periodo compreso tra la Battaglia di Campaldino (11 Giugno 1289) e quella di Altopascio (23 settembre 1325), risponde alla volontà di evidenziare un momento storico cruciale per la Toscana, sia dal punto di vista storico/militare che culturale. Infatti gli anni che vanno dal 1289 al 1325 vedono cambiamenti importanti nel corredo dell'uomo d'arme del tempo, con l'introduzione delle prime forme parziali di armatura a piastre e di nuovi elementi difensivi quali schinieri, guanti e altre parti di armatura. È in quegli anni, in seguito alla battaglia di Campaldino, che ha inizio l'egemonia di Firenze sulle altre città toscane. La Compagnia offre un quadro storico mutevole e dinamico, vivido e realistico, in cui le protezioni di cuoio bollito e la cotta di maglia convivono con le innovazioni tecnologiche che caratterizzeranno l'uomo d'arme dei secoli successivi.

Contacts:
E-mail: antichipopoli@gmail.com
Website: http://www.antichipopoli.it/

Pisa Ghibellina

Il gruppo storico Pisa Ghibellina nacque dalla volontà di riscoprire e tramandare la storia basso medievale della Città di Pisa; in quest'ottica, l'associazione si propone di rappresentare una compagnia detta "venticinquina" delle milizie comunali Pisane, che a differenza di altri comuni dell'epoca come Firenze o Siena, non arruolava gli effettivi sul modello della leva militare, nel terziere o sestiere, ma era legata, tramite vincoli di stampo feudale e/o familiare, ad alcune famiglie di antica schiatta che dominavano sui quartieri della città, formando delle consorterie nobiliari. Nello specifico la compagnia che si ricostruisce è quella appartenuta alla consorteria dei Conti di Donoratico Della Gheradesca, i quali dominavano sul quartiere a sud dell'Arno chiamato Chinzica. Il periodo storico verso cui ci siamo orientati va dagli inizi del XIII secolo, passando per la Battaglia di Montaperti avvenuta il 4 settembre 1260, fino alla Battaglia di Montecatini svoltasi il 29 agosto 1315. L'associazione Pisa Ghibellina si occupa dello studio del combattimento medievale con tutte le tipologie di armi e armature che venivano usate durante le battaglie del XIII secolo e primo quarto del XIV secolo, ricostruisce abiti e suppellettili, ha realizzato autonomamente il proprio accampamento (cucendo le tende e ricreando la cucina mobile), svolge vita da campo attenendosi il più possibile a ciò che poteva esserci allora e mangiando esclusivamente ricette dell'epoca con ingredienti che si potevano trovare nel basso medioevo in Italia (escludendo perciò quanto venne introdotto con la scoperta dell'America). L'associazione e i suoi membri si attengono scrupolosamente a questi dettami cogliendo così l'opportunità di capire a fondo, attraverso "l'archeologia sperimentale e ricostruttiva", come doveva essere la vita in un accampamento e/o in un realtà castellana o di una città basso medievale.

Contacts:
E-mail: flyingwing@hotmail.it
Website: http://www.pisaghibellina.it/

Sjórvaldar Vikings

Sjórvaldar Vikings are a 501.(c)3 non-profit organization whose primary focus is dedicated to enriching the educational experience through immersive living history. Sjórvaldar was founded with a shared interest and passion for the history, crafts, battle elements of all things Scandinavian, with the intention and commitment to share it with the public with as much authenticity as possible. Members aim to depict a mobile, seasonal camp/temporary village complete with living quarters, work spaces, and recreational areas. The village not only showcases the lifestyle and culture of the period, but also the harsher and battle ready aspects of life in what was know as the Viking age, specifically the 10th century. With a thoughtful training regimen and regular training sessions, members learn the ins and outs of planning and performing a safe, entertaining and as realistic as possible combat display, without jeopardizing our personal safety. At our events we strive to a high standard of presentation, historical accuracy and attention to detail with all endeavours, either with active demonstrations or displays. Our presentations are based upon archaeological research and literary research. From weaving, to blacksmithing, to woodworking and everything in between, members enjoy sharing their skills with and educating the public by demonstrating live period crafts as they would have been practised during the Viking age.

Contacts:
E-mail: sjorvaldarvikings@gmail.com
Website: https://www.sjorvaldar.com/
Facebook: https://www.facebook.com/sjorvaldar/

Index